UNDERSTANDING
THE
I CHING

UNDERSTANDING
THE
I CHING

Restoring a Brilliant, Ancient Culture

Alfred Huang
edited by Daniel Nesbitt

Library of Congress Cataloging in Publication Data:

ISBN: 1493735632
ISBN 13: 9781493735631
Library of Congress Control Number: 2014903394
CreateSpace Independent Publishing Platform
North Charleston, South Carolina

Dedicated to Beloved Mother, Grandma and Grandpa

To my dearly beloved Mother, who sacrificed her life at age twenty.

Her little boy caught scarlet fever and could not open his mouth to eat. Kneeling down on the ground before the little child, protesting against all the doctors' serious warnings, she cried and screamed, insisting on feeding her eighteen-month-old child mouth to mouth... After three days she met with scarlet fever herself and passed away.

Then, the child continued to be fed mouth to mouth by his exceedingly beloved Grandma. Over time, his Grandpa patiently guided him to a valuable and meaningful life... In this way, the child was able to grow up.

I owe my life to their sincerity, sacrifice and generosity.

Alfred
With daughter
Margaret, kow tow

Acknowledgments

In the Acknowledgments of *The Complete I Ching*, published by Inner Traditions International in 1998, I told a story:

> It is not rare to find horses able to cover a thousand li a day, but Bo Le 百乐 is rare. In the late period of the Spring and Autumn Annals (770 – 476 B.C.), there was a man, Bo Le, who was adept in looking at a horse to judge its worth. Among a herd of horses he was able to point out the one that was able to cover a thousand li a day. (Li is a Chinese unit of length equivalent to half a kilometer.)

The story suggests that, without Bo Le, horses able to cover a thousand li a day often go unrecognized. At that time, Bo Le was Mr. Jon Graham, the acquisitions editor of Inner Traditions International. His enthusiastic effort in conferring with his company about publishing my book reminds me of this ancient tale.

But now, as I am ninety-three, I have much experience in identifying "horses" that are able to cover a thousand li a day. Here I am appreciatively acknowledging the "horse," that has participated in bringing this project to completion.

To my surprise, the "steed" is Dan Nesbitt. With a professional background as a software engineer and an expert in technologies ranging from semiconductors to medical devices to mobile app development, he may seem an unlikely, if not strange, choice as my editor. After I was introduced to him by a common friend, I found out that he is much more than a computer whiz. He is a teacher, mentor and leadership coach, a martial artist, a scholar and an entrepreneur. I never doubted his intellect, but still I was very surprised when we started working together and I got to experience his editing talent. Dan is serious, conscientious, careful, painstaking and responsible. In his editing, he masterfully balances literary precision with his commitment to staying true to the content and honoring the author's expertise. Like a true martial artist, he wields his literary sword with skill and finesse. For me, he is the best editor I have ever worked with.

I would also like to extend my profound thanks to Regina Sara Ryan for her highly professional copy-editing. Her extensive editing experience and depth of scholarship elevated the quality of the entire manuscript.

Contents

Editor's Introduction by Daniel Nesbitt   xi

Preface   xix

Chapter 1 – The Singularity of the I Ching   1
The Three *I*. King Wen's Contributions. Divination and Philosophy /
Yin and Yang. The Two Schools. *I* of the Past Hundred Years.

Chapter 2 – The Soul of the I Ching   10
Seeking Harmony. Grandpa's Instructions.

Chapter 3 – The System of the I Ching   19
Eight Trigrams. Three Powers – Heaven, Earth, Humanity. Two Phases
– Upper and Lower Gua / Inner and Outer / Subjective and Objective.
Seating Arrangement – Positions of Lines. Their Functions / Sequence /
Names / Proper Place . . . The Essence of Zhou I.

Chapter 4 – The Host of the Gua   32
Appropriate Use of the I Ching. **The Upper Canon**– Hosts of.
The Lower Canon – Hosts of.

Chapter 5 – The Sequence of the I Ching   53
King Wen's Philosophy. Eight Primary Gua. Hidden Balance of
the Gua. Hidden Balance of the Yao. Unchangeable Truth – Dealing
with Time and Situation.

Chapter 6 – The Gateway of the I Ching   64
The Source of Chinese Culture. The Tao of Heaven. Words / Symbols.
The Essence of the Second Hexagram. The Tao of Earth.

Chapter 7 – Yuan Heng Li Zhen   79
The Decision of the First Hexagram. The Tao of Heaven and Tao of
Humanity. Yuan – Heng – Li – Zhen. **Seven Hexagrams Containing
These Four** in Their Decisions: Initiating, Responding, Beginning,
Following, Approaching, Without Falsehood, Abolishing the Old.

Chapter 8 – The Judgment of the I Ching   93
8 Judgments in the I Ching. **Positions of the Yao**: Correct/ Incorrect
// Central / Not Central // Responding / Corresponding // Carrying /
Mounting // Departing / Arriving
Humbleness is Extraordinary. The Decision of the Second Gua.

Chapter 9 – Nine Hexagrams for Character Formation   106
Fulfillment / Humbleness / Turning Back / Long Lasting /
Decreasing / Increasing /
Exhausting / Replenishing / Proceeding. Three Statements of
Confucius on Character Formation.

Millennium Time Capsule Text by Master Alfred Huang,   114
October 2000

Epilogue by Regina Sara Ryan   117

About the Author   119

Editor's Introduction

by Daniel Nesbitt

The I Ching is a monumental book. Like the headwaters of two mighty rivers, it is a seminal text of both the Confucian and Taoist traditions. It is the underpinning of Chinese culture and society, encapsulating the wisdom of benevolent government and laying the foundations for early forms of the Chinese nation state. It also shaped the nature of modern Chinese thought through promotion of the concepts of symbolic thinking and the understanding of generalizations through analogy. The I Ching is a book for everyone. Through the ages, rulers, ministers, advisers, scholars, warriors and common folk have all found it to be a reliable source of wisdom and insight into their circumstances, and a guide to their conduct.

My journey with the I Ching and Master Alfred Huang began in late October of 2012. I was commencing a three-week silent retreat in a pickup-style camper on a remote hillside of a farm in the Monashee mountain range of British Columbia. I took one piece of study material into my retreat, Master Alfred's book, *The Complete I Ching*. I had a long-standing interest in oriental philosophy and for some time had wanted to study the I Ching.

I kept a simple routine, to bed at sundown (around 7 PM at that time of year), rising again in the preternatural stillness at 3 AM, sitting in meditation until the first traces of daylight appeared in the sky. As the sun rose, I would bundle up and emerge from the camper to watch the sunrise slowly creep up the mountain slopes and the landscape emerge from the darkness. Flocks of crows would begin their daily migration overhead from their rookery to their daytime territory. A curious fox would often emerge from the margin of the field to check me out, and then shyly retreat to the forest when I returned its inquisitive gaze. A herd of deer roamed the adjacent field, the sound of their hooves on the ground providing background ambience. At the end of the day, I would stand outside and watch the sunset. The landscape faded back into darkness, the crows flew the reciprocal of their morning flight path and I retreated to the camper for a simple dinner and sleep.

Also, amongst the natural noises in the environment, I heard the roar of logging trucks charging up the valley in the pre-dawn darkness, while the flicker of their high-beam headlights in the far-distance cast scintillating highlights on my surroundings. They raced to a woodlot on a not-too-distant hillside where, even at that hour, they rushed to harvest lumber prior to the onset of winter in the mountains. The sound of massive machinery ripping through the forest at a ferocious pace was daunting. Above the rumble of diesel engines, the high-pitched shriek of chain saws invaded my hoped-for silent cocoon. What a powerful reminder of human impact on nature! As I looked down on the valley below, and indeed on many of the surrounding hillsides, the patchwork remnants of other logging operations at varying stages of regrowth resembled a mangy street dog's coat. Almost a hundred years prior, the entire pristine valley full of old growth trees had been set on fire by a rancher wanting more space for ranching cattle. These and other potent reminders of the fragility of nature and the impermanent relationship we modern humans have to comfort, survival and safety were everywhere One day, sometime after the herd of deer passed through the clearing and beyond to a trail leading to a logging road that bordered the farm property, the silence was punctuated by a series of rifle shots. I didn't see the deer or hear their hoof-fall for the remainder of my retreat.

Within my inner landscape, the long days of meditative and mantric practice shed harsh light on the manifestations within that lead to the manifestation without of conflicts between people and between humankind and nature. It caused me to question the independence I assumed between conflicts in my inner world and the outer world. It made me wonder also about the greater conflicts in the sweep of human history, how many wars and other violations were a product of the inner dissonance of powerful and influential people through the ages. How does such dissonance influence our treatment of our natural environment and our understanding of our place within it?

Inside my camper during the day, I poured over Master Alfred's *The Complete I Ching*. His descriptions of the gua and their elucidation of the harmonious and disharmonious interplay of Heaven, Earth and Humankind was brought to life by the circumstances around me. The rhythms of day and night; the changing moods of the landscape in varying weather and time of day; the activities of the animals . . . all was greatly amplified and contrasted by the interventions of modern technology. And all echoed and resonated somehow with Master Alfred's lively engagements of the gua. Through his remarkable treatment, I had an access to the continuum of human experience, back to antiquity, which paradoxically also illuminated my appreciation and insight into the present day. I was enormously grateful for the teaching I received from him.

For Master Alfred, the study of the I Ching has provided the backdrop to his entire life. His study was not just a scholarly pursuit, but also a personal apprenticeship with great masters, starting with his grandfather – who began instructing him on the principles of the I Ching from his sixteenth birthday. Indeed, the wisdom of I Ching was key to his survival through the twenty-two years he was incarcerated by the Chinese Communist government in prisons and labor camps due to his Christian background, dissenting from the policy of class struggle and for the "crime" of studying and believing the Taoist and Confucian traditions.

His book, *The Complete I Ching*, has been praised as a masterwork in the field and celebrated widely for its success in conveying the timeless wisdom of the I Ching to English speaking audiences. Due to the great expanse of time from the composition of the I Ching to the present day, there are great differences in today's readers, stemming from modern culture, which demand a bridge from faithful translations of the text of the I Ching, to a full and complete understanding of its history, influences, and required background subjects. This book, *Understanding The I Ching*, is a text written to bridge the ancient times of the composition of the I Ching with the modern age.

The I Ching is primarily of symbolic origins. There were two parallel sets of symbols: the unique, six-line, hexagrams of each gua and the pictographic symbols chosen to represent the essential nature of each gua. Each of the sixty-four gua represents a time-situation, an overall characterization of the fluid and dynamic transition from past, to present and to future circumstances.

The original text was written in ancient Chinese pictographs, abandoned long ago, which considerably predate the other pictographs of modern usage. All the writings that have followed are essentially elaborations and interpretations of these original pictographs. In completing his older work, *The Complete I Ching*, Master Alfred first revisited the original pictographs of the I Ching text and translated them to modern Chinese characters. To the best of his knowledge, all other English translations of the I Ching rely on interpretations of derivative works, written in relatively modern language.

This current book is intended for people who have invested considerable time in studying an authentic translation of the I Ching, and who are seeking a deeper understanding of its interpretation. The book is organized as a series in chapters, which are essentially somewhat overlapping essays on in-depth topics of the I Ching compiled together to provide a well rounded, reinforced understanding of these deep principles. Master Alfred enhances the reader's understanding by circling back over critical subject matter as a deliberate means to heighten the teaching potential of the text. It seeks to impart to the reader a background in topics that are not commonly available to English language audiences. For example, Master Alfred spends considerable effort in this book elucidating the nature of the first two gua of the I Ching, Heaven (Qian) and Earth (Kun). These two gua are truly the gateway to the I Ching, revealing the primordial nature of masculine and feminine, yin and yang, in the ongoing, eternal process of creation and manifestation. A deep understanding of the principles of these two gua is essential for a profound mastery of the content of the I Ching.

Additionally, Master Alfred has devoted an entire chapter to the four characters, yuan, heng, li and zhen, which comprise the Decision of Qian, the first hexagram. Together and separately, these four characters have several important interpretations, which represent guiding principles throughout the text of the I Ching.

The basic symbolic nature of the I Ching gives rise to two separate yet related interpretations, much like modern physics describes the relationship between particles and waves in quantum mechanics. As one aspect of the I Ching is the idealized relationships between Heaven, Earth and humans, it naturally follows that one aspect of the study of the I Ching is that typically referred to as the "School of Morality and Reason." This school is concerned with an interpretation of the I Ching from the unique perspective of a human being. The other complimentary aspect of the study of the I Ching is tradition- ally referred to as the "Symbol and Number School," which employs the im- personal, numerological relationships of lines within and between hexagrams to reveal an understanding of the I Ching that is concealed otherwise. From this paradigm, many aspects of study of the I Ching – such as the sequence of the gua, transitions between them and the beautiful, often unrecognized, symmetries of the hexagrams, which seem otherwise random – are revealed to have a hidden order that further illuminates their interpretations. In this book, Master Alfred gives attention to both schools of study of the I Ching.

In order to understand intuitively the transitions between the time-sit- uations represented by the gua, one must have a thorough grasp of the con- struction of the sixty-four hexagrams. Each of the six-line positions in the hexagrams has an individual character and a relationship to each of the other positions. One must also have a comprehensive understanding of the place- ment and significance of the host of the hexagram, the dominant line (or in some cases pair of lines), which is the governing influence of the nature of a gua. Master Alfred explicates this topic in depth in this current volume.

The great master Confucius gave tremendous emphasis to the subject of the I Ching and character formation. In fact, he devoted the entire seventh chapter of his book *The Great Treatise* to the subject. Following in the tradi- tion of Confucius, Master Alfred believes fiercely, as he notes in his Preface here, that the use of the I Ching for the purpose of divination is not the high- est use of the text. Instead, the I Ching is to be taken as a living reference of conduct appropriate for the highest moral and ethical standards in any given life circumstance. In troubled and uncertain times, the I Ching provides a ready source of wisdom for consultation by leaders and followers alike, at all stations of society.

It is a remarkable situation that, some 5,000 years on, the I Ching continues to light a path forward for human civilization as relevant as at any time in its long and storied history. Despite its recent suppression in China during the period of the Cultural Revolution, the I Ching has emerged again as an exalted source of ancient wisdom for leading humanity into the future.

Master Alfred writes compellingly and optimistically about the arc of humanity's future that he sees as a progression of spiritual growth and profound harmony in the coming centuries. The kind of global transformation that Master Alfred envisions for humankind as a whole is predicated on an individual-by-individual decision to live from the principles of kindness, righteousness, harmony and uprightness. The I Ching and Master Alfred Huang's brilliant commentary on it contained in this work provide a ready guide for that personal journey.

为天地立心
为生民立命
为先圣继絶学
为后世开太平

—— 张载 ——

Set up a divine heart
Between heaven and earth;

Bringing out meaningful lives
To the living.

Continue the unsurpassed learning
Of the past;

Creating eternal peace
For the future.

– Zhang Zai –

Preface

I

This book, *Understanding the I Ching*, with the sub-title *Restoring A Brilliant, Ancient Culture*, is truly an introduction to another, future book, *The Comprehensive I Ching*, which I am planning to write. Being a native Chinese, I revere the I Ching as much as Westerners respect the Holy Bible. For this reason, when I translated the I Ching from the original Chinese into English in my older work, *The Complete I Ching*, I strictly followed what Confucius taught, "Narrate, but do not write 述而不作." This teaching instructs that, when conveying another's thoughts, simply narrate; do not add any of your own opinions. As a result, *The Complete I Ching* has been hailed as a modern masterpiece. It was judged by *Intuition* magazine to be "superior in nearly every respect to the earlier English versions." The book was also lauded by Professor Jack M. Balkin of Yale Law School, who wrote in his book, *The Laws of Change – I Ching and The Philosophy of Life*, "It is perhaps the finest traditional translation that has appeared since Wilhelm / Baynes."

But in reality, most of my relatives and many of my friends told me: "It seems easy to understand superficially, but it is still hard to comprehend its subtleties."

Following serious meditation on this, gradually I realized there is a tremendous difference in the life experience of people from 3,000 years ago, when the I Ching was composed, to those in the present day. In order to assist people to understand the profundity of the I Ching, there is a need of books *about* the I Ching, like the ancient Eight Wings, as well as translations of the I Ching in concise form.

The I Ching reveals an ancient culture that honors Heaven 尊天, esteems the Earth 敬地, and expresses love for the people 爱人. It espouses a culture of seeking harmony 和谐 – seeking harmony with Heaven 与天和, seeking harmony with Earth 与地和, seeking harmony with people 与人和, and seeking harmony with one's own body and mind 与身心和. It also extols the maxim, "Within the four seas, all will be brothers 四海之内, 皆兄弟也." The I Ching elucidated a culture of practicing "benevolent government 仁政," which strictly followed what the ancients pointed out that, "To govern is to rectify 政者, 正也." "When a king's (in modern times a ruler's) personal conduct is correct, the government is effective without coercion 其身正, 不令而行. If the ruler's personal conduct is not correct, he may issue orders, but they will not be followed 其身不正, 虽令不从." As a result, "When a country is well governed, poverty and oppression are things to be ashamed of 邦有道, 贫且贱焉, 耻也; when a country is ill governed, riches and honors are things to be ashamed of. 邦无道, 富且贵焉, 耻也."

Adhering to the tradition of honoring Heaven, the Chinese embrace a viewpoint of, "Death and life are predetermined appointments 死生有命; riches and honors depend upon Heaven 富贵在天." In relying totally upon the will of Heaven, the Chinese thus believe in retribution 报应, that one deserves a fate according to how one behaves, either for good or evil. They are familiar with the concept, "As you sow, so will you reap 种瓜得瓜, 种豆得豆." For obtaining good fortune and avoiding misfortune, they acted according to what the I Ching instructed. As yuan 元, heng 亨, li 利, and zhen 贞 were the guiding principles of the I Ching, the ancient Chinese developed these qualities long ago, which nowadays are interpreted as kindness, righteousness, harmony and uprightness. Through the process of putting oneself in the place of another 推己及人, people learned to treat others as one would like to be treated. In this way, a moral society had been unconsciously formed. This is what the ancients said: "People are doing it every day but without being aware of it."

On the other hand, the "super men 君子" of ancient times – nowadays known as "people of absolute integrity," stressed studying the I Ching, especially after the I Ching had been assigned as required reading for the imperial examinations during the Western Han dynasty, about 3,000 years ago. First of all, they stressed cultivating moral character. They strictly followed the teaching of the first and the second gua, Initiating and Responding, to keep themselves "vital without ceasing" and "to enrich their virtue to sustain all beings." For preparing to be a "super man" there is a fifty-three-item code of conduct that should be followed.

Carefully and thoroughly, they studied how King Wen and the Duke of Zhou demonstrated "benevolent government," especially the qualities of acting as a "benevolent king." For these great men, keeping abreast of public feeling 考察民情; improving people's quality of living 改善民生, as well as eliminating corruption and incompetence 清除腐败, were the priorities. They assisted the ruler in taking care of people's birth, aging, sickness and death 生老病死, allowing people to live and to work in peace 安居乐业, appreciating that people need rest to maintain their strength 休养生息. This allowed people to accept things as they are, abide by the law 安常处顺, be content, take responsibility for themselves 安份守己, and resolve to never be the cause of others' physical, mental, or psychological sufferings 折磨百姓 . . . People were able to think and to talk freely 言论自由, and to be carefree and unfettered 逍遥自在. There was a pet phrase saying, "There is no government official to be feared 不怕官; only their unreasonable control 只怕管."

Nevertheless, "Falling into a pit, gain a wit 吃一堑, 长一智." I thoroughly believe that the Divine 上苍 is allowing the Chinese to experience the consequences of a living where there is no honor given to Heaven, no esteem to Earth, and no love expressed to people.

After Communists took over China in 1949, a philosophy of "man should conquer nature 人定胜天" and a policy of "class struggle 阶级斗争" was carried out. The masses were educated, agitated and aroused with slogans of "fighting with Heaven 与天斗,""fighting with Earth 与地斗," "fighting with people 与人斗" . . . "what a great pleasure 何其乐也!" Then, a strategy the Chinese call "a monk holding an umbrella 和尚打伞" was carried out, which hints at a state of lack of respect for the law and a lack of reverence for Heaven, as there is an umbrella obstructing the view of Heaven.[1]

After having "gained a wit," Chinese people are cherishing their ancient culture more than ever. They hold fast to what the I Ching taught, that, "When things go beyond the extreme, a change will come 物极必变"; and, "After the darkest period, the dawn is near at hand. 否极泰来."

Consider that, amongst the world population, one out of four is a Chinese. As most Chinese treasure their brilliant, traditional culture of honoring Heaven, esteeming Earth, expressing love towards the people and seeking harmony – what a substantial foundation of world peace and blissful living for people of all the world they could create!

As a student of the I Ching, I do not worry about abolishing the old 革旧, but instead, I focus on establishing the new 鼎新. I deeply believe that a "modern benevolent government," which is the design of the Divine 上苍, will soon appear at the dawn of the twenty-first century.

With this sentiment as inspiration, this book of *Understanding the I Ching – Restoring A Brilliant, Ancient Culture* is written.

II

In the Preface of *The Complete I Ching*, I wrote:

> . . . According to the I Ching, every country has its destiny, and every person has his or her fate, but everyone still has the freedom to make their own choices. Of the four scholars I studied with – Master Yin, Dr. Ting, Professor Liu, and I – I was the youngest. The others were of my father's generation. Being with them, I realized that I had much to learn and experience. . . .

---

1 "A monk holding an umbrella" hints that the ruler of the country disrespects the law. As monks have a shaved head, they have no hair. In Chinese, hair and law share the same pronunciation, which suggests a state of lack respect for the law or reverence for Heaven.

Although we knew that after the long night there would come the dawn; the dawn did not come soon. In two years Master Yin and Dr. Ting passed away one after the other. Professor Liu lost his desire to live. He attempted suicide several times. Although I encouraged him to persevere, deep in my heart I thought that those who had died were the blessed ones. They had ended their sufferings and were able to enjoy everlasting peace. Those who were still alive had to face every kind of unimaginable suffering and strive for survival. But, from the bottom of my heart, I chose to live, to live as long as I could and see the destiny of China, no matter what hardships might ensue . . .

On the 26th of December 2013, when I was already ninety-two years old, it was the 120th birthday of the late Mao Ze Dong. Countless places were planning to spend several million Chinese yuan for occasions of extraordinarily grand and solemn ceremonies in his honor.

On that day I was quietly staying at home, sitting in my study meditating, and recalling that Mao continuously advocated his idea of New Democracy 新民主主义 into the 1940s. In this he promised that peasants would have their own lands 于农民以土地, intellectuals would have their freedom 于知识分子以自由, those who owned industrial and commercial enterprises would have ownership of their development 于工商业者以发展, workers would have their leadership authority 于工人以领导权, and all Chinese would have what the American President Lincoln declared: "Government of the people, by the people, and for the people 于所有的中国人以 "美国林肯总统的民有,民治,民享." In addition, he promised the equivalent of the American President Franklin D. Roosevelt's "Four Freedoms," 和美国罗斯福总统的四大自由 – "freedom of speech 表达意志的自由, freedom of worship 崇拜的自由, freedom from want 不虞匮乏的自由, and freedom from fear 免除恐惧的自由." Even until September of 1949, Mao still made great effort to use his New Democracy as bait to negotiate with all Democratic parties to achieve a "Common Political Agenda 共同纲领."

However, what Abraham Lincoln advocated was, "All men are created equal." On the 10th of December 1948, the UN Universal Declaration of Human Rights further extended Lincoln's statement to proclaim. "All human beings are born free and equal in dignity and rights . . ." But, after taking over China in 1949, Mao divided Chinese people into nine classes – namely, land lords 地主, rich peasants 富农, counter-revolutionaries 反革命分子, bad elements 坏分子, rightists 右派分子, traitors 叛徒, spies 特务, capitalists 走资派, and "disgusting" intellectuals 臭知识分子.

Once Confucius' favorite student, Zi Gong 子贡, asked the question, "What constitutes the superior man?"

Confucius replied 曰, "He acts before he speaks 先行其言, and afterwards speaks according to his actions 而后从之." On another occasion, the Master said 孔子曰, "At first, my way with men was to hear their words, and give them credit for their conduct 始我与人也, 听其言而信其行. Now my way is to hear their words, and look at their conduct. 今我于人也, 听其言而观其行. It is from Yu that I have learned to make this change 于予与改是."

Once again, Zi Gong asked the Master, 子贡再问曰: "What qualities must a man possess to entitle him to be an officer? 何如斯可谓之士矣?"

The Master said, 曰, "To be sincere in what they say 言必信, and to be responsible for what they do 行必果." The Master said again 孔子曰, "From the old, death has been the lot of all men 自古皆有死; if the people *have no faith in their rulers*, there is *no standing for the state* 民无信不立." The Master continued 子曰: "When good government prevails in a state 邦有道, language may be lofty and bold, and actions the same 危言危行. When bad government prevails 邦无道, language may be lofty and bold, but the associated actions may fall short of the rhetoric 危行言逊."

III

As a native Chinese, I consider I Ching as the Bible of China. As water has its source and trees their roots, I Ching is the source and the roots of the Chinese culture. I consider the *Eight Wings*, written by Confucius and his disciples, the best interpretation of the I Ching, because Confucius and his disciples lived only 500 years following the emergence of King Wen's I Ching.

I believe I Ching is a collection of the countless experiences and wisdom of the ancient folks. These were accumulated through thousands of years and passed down orally generation after generation. Once King Wen had gathered all of the best of these influences, plus his own life experiences and philosophy, he composed the I Ching of the Zhou dynasty.

When I was sixteen years of age, grandpa, my mentor, introduced me to the field of I Ching. He talked about six dragons flying in the sky and a mare galloping across the vast plain in the first and the second hexagrams, Qian 乾 and Kun 坤, of the I Ching. In great detail he explained the four Chinese characters yuan 元, heng 亨, li 利 and zhen 贞, the guiding principles of the I Ching.

He told me that most people considered I Ching as a manual of fortune telling, but actually it was a book guiding people in practicing truthful thinking and proper behavior. Everyone who thinks and acts according to what I Ching instructs is a superior man or woman, or, as we would say nowadays, a gentleman or gentlewoman. In living according to the principles of the I Ching, they would experience good fortune and avoid misfortune.

Grandpa also pointed out that I Ching directs people in establishing a positive attitude of life that can be expressed as, "Heaven acts with vitality and persistence, the superior person keeps himself vital without ceasing"; and "Earth's nature is responding and submissive, the superior person enriches his virtue to sustain all beings." It is the same as what Lao Zi 老子 said, "Men follow Earth 人法地, Earth follows Heaven 地法天, Heaven follows the Tao 天法道, and the Tao follows Nature 道法自然."

Once grandpa talked about the soul of the I Ching. Grandpa said, "The soul of the I Ching is Seeking Harmony 同人, which is the thirteenth gua. I Ching's main theme is seeking harmony, which should be pursued with absolute unselfishness and with the best interests of the majority in mind."

When I was put into prison in 1966, it was a horrible place, which I could not have even imagined. How was I to deal with all the other people around me at that time? I remembered what the I Ching taught and what Confucius explained. The Master had said, "I have heard that the superior man is not a partisan 我闻君子不党." The Master went on to say 又曰: "The superior man is restrained and never contentious, gregarious but not cliquish. 君子矜而不争, 群而不党." Thank God, during twenty-two years of hard labor and confinement in the prison, I was able to never betray any of my friends and never report to the authorities against anyone in or outside of the prison 检举揭发, especially when the persons who were sent by the government to interview me in the prison asked me about others' words and deeds against the government or the party. I felt extremely happy that it was my only chance to speak *freely* according to my *free will* to "report" to the government all of my friends' good words and deeds.

The most valuable harvest in the twenty-two years of a tortured life of confinement was relying on the Divine's guidance all the time, like being a female horse – "Predetermining; loses. Following; gets a master" in the second hexagram of the I Ching, Responding.

Grandpa used to say, regarding the submission of the female horse, "One should obey what the Divine guides."

I still remember the day I was released from the prison. As soon as I stepped out of the gate, I said a prayer: "Dear God, I passed the examination!"

I never thought it was a suffering, but, instead, I regarded it as training!

*   *   *

In the fifteen years or so since 1998, when *The Complete I Ching* was published, people have been most interested in asking the following questions:

The first, "How often do you use the I Ching for the purpose of divining?"

To which I generally reply: "Not very often! – A few times a year; only for extremely important decisions. But I examine myself on yuan, heng, li and zhen frequently."

Second, "How did you get the strength to survive during those awful years in prison?" My answer: "I suffered joyfully!"

And the third, "How do you deal with the one who made false charges against you?"

I say: "It's easy! – If I cannot forgive, I just forget. That's all!"

1

周易的特质
The Singularity of the I Ching

The earliest precursors of the I Ching, the oldest book in the world, appeared around 5,000 years ago. It is believed that I Ching gave birth to Chinese culture.

At the very beginning, there were only symbols in I Ching, no "characters," as these had not yet been invented. And, no one named it "I Ching"; people just called it "*I*," which signified easy to understand and easy to follow. (*I* pronounced *yi*, or ee as easy; not *ai*.)

An age-old legend recounts that, during remote antiquity around the beginning of the New Stone Age, Fu Xi 伏牺, a legendary king, upon observing the "characters of birds and beasts," invented the pictographs of the eight trigrams 八卦. Later on, he was inspired by one of the eight trigrams, li ☲ to teach people how to weave nets to catch fish and hunt animals.

The Three *I*

In the history of China there were three *I*: namely, the Lian Shan I 连山易, the Gui Zang I 归藏易, and the 周易 Zhou I. The first one, Lian Shan I, was written in the Xia 夏 dynasty (2100 B.C. – 1600 B.C.), about 4,000 years ago, by Emperor Yan 炎帝, another legendary king. It was said that Emperor Yan was inspired by the symbol of the forty-second gua Yi ䷩ 益 to invent the plough, thus enlivening agriculture. He also tasted hundreds of herbs, thereby discovering the curative virtues of plants. The second one, Gui Zang I 归藏易, was written in the Shang 商 dynasty (1600 B.C. – 1100 B.C.), about 3,500 years ago, by the Yellow Emperor 黄帝. It is believed that the Yellow Emperor originated the calendar system and invented the compass. The third one, Zhou I 周易, was written by King Wen 文王 at the intersection of the Shang 商 dynasty and the Zhou 周 dynasty (1100 B.C. – 771 B.C.), about 3,000 years ago.

Strictly speaking, when we mention I Ching, we denote the three *I* 三易. If we mention Zhou I 周易, we refer to the book we are now using written by King Wen. The other two *I* were not passed down.

While most people think Zhou I is an abbreviation for "I Ching of the Zhou dynasty," many others do not. Their disagreement is based on the consideration that Lian Shan I and Gui Zang I did not base their titles on the names of their respective dynasties – Xia and Shang – as "Xia I" or "Shang I" but instead, on the symbols of the first gua in their books. The symbol of the first gua of Lian Shan I is Mountain ☶ above and Mountain ☶ below, which signifies clouds drifting out of mountains in succession. This is considered symbolic of connection or linkage. Thus, people were saying, "The Way of Xia dynasty is linking, linking 夏道连连." At that time, as it was a hunting era, people were exploring and being inspired by mountains and forests.

At the time Gui Zang I was written, it was in the context of a matrilineal society 母系社会. The symbol of the first gua of Gui Zang I was Earth ☷ above and Earth ☷ below. People had already entered into the agricultural era; they had already conceived of the idea that all beings in the end would return back to the earth and be buried underneath. As they honored Earth as Great Mother, so too they placed the image of Earth at the beginning in their I Ching. They were fond of saying, "The way of Yin was qin, qin 殷道亲亲," which means "the way of Yin dynasty is intimacy, intimacy" – "intimacy with mother." (The Yin dynasty is actually the same as the Shang dynasty, which is why it is usually called the "Yin-Shang dynasty."

When King Wen wrote the book of *I*, society had already transitioned to a patrilineal model 父系社会. King Wen was inspired by the phenomena of yin and yang. Thus, King Wen put Qian ☰ 乾 and Kun ☷ 坤 – Initiating and Responding – at the beginning of his book. Thus, the first two gua, Initiating ☰ and Responding ☷, became the Introduction of the book; and the last two gua, Ji Ji ䷾ 既济 and Wei Ji ䷿ 未济, comprise the Conclusion. Ji Ji ䷾ 既济 means Already Fulfilled and Wei Ji ䷿ 未济 means Not Yet Fulfilled.

With regards to the interpretation of the title of Zhou I 周易, the meaning of the Chinese character 周 zhou also means "to be fully prepared," "to be thoroughly thought over," "to be comprehensively considered," and furthermore "to go round and begin again." For all these reasons, those who oppose considering 周易 Zhou I as an abbreviation for the I Ching of the Zhou dynasty are of the opinion that zhou should be a descriptive term of how King Wen prepared himself "fully," "thoroughly," and "comprehensively" for writing on the topic of the I Ching. Most of all, they think that zhou describes one of the main themes of the book, which expounds on the truth that "all things between Heaven and Earth go around and begin again . . ."

Furthermore, King Wen then considered most significantly that the essence of Zhou I is Seeking Highest Harmony 太和, which will be fully discussed in the second chapter of this book, *The Soul of the I Ching*. While I am composing this one, *Understanding the I Ching*, I cannot stop thinking that, "The Way of Zhou is centralizing and rectifying 周道中正 ! "

King Wen's Contributions

Let us consider what King Wen actually did in recomposing the *I*.

First: King Wen revised the names of the sixty-four gua making them more aligned with the nature of the symbols. For example, in the Gui Zang I, the I Ching of the Shang dynasty, the image of Ru 溽, humid or damp, was Water ☵ above and Heaven ☰ below. King Wen made it Rain ☵ above and Heaven ☰ below. Another example, he revised the 兼 (meaning to double, unite, connect) to 谦, which means humble.

Second: King Wen made improvements on what had already been achieved in the other two *I* by cutting out unnecessary details of divination, making the Decisions more understandable to readers. He rewrote the Decisions, explaining the names and the significance of the gua. In this way, he makes the divination easier "to comprehend through analogy 触类旁通." That is, after grasping the meaning of a typical example, the reader will then be able to grasp the meaning of a whole category of related scenarios. As a result, King Wen made "comprehending through analogy 触类旁通" a mature way of Chinese thinking.

Third: King Wen re-arranged the sequence of the sixty-four gua. According to the first gua of Gui Zang I, it is Earth ☷ above and Earth ☷ below, which reflects that people of Yin dynasty thought highly of the maternal blood relationship and believed that Earth created the myriad beings. King Wen therefore rearranged Initiating (Heaven) and Responding (Earth) as the first and second gua. Besides emphasizing the yin-yang phenomena, this reflected the attachment of the people of the Zhou dynasty to paternal blood relationship and respected the unity of Heaven and Humanity 天人合一. It also underscored the idea of "Heaven being exalted and Earth supportive," as well as the idea of "the male being dominant and the female submissive."

In addition to recomposing the I Ching, King Wen displaced the Yin-Shang dynasty, which meant not only a change of human affairs but also a significant revolution in thinking and beliefs.

Divination and Philosophy / Yin and Yang

At the beginning, I Ching was a book of divination; it belonged to the shamanic civilization 巫术文化. On the other hand, The Commentary of the I Ching, which is a book explaining the I Ching philosophically, fits more into the category of Confucian philosophy.

While the I Ching took shape between the Yin dynasty and the Zhou dynasty (1100 B.C. – 221 B.C.), about 3,000 years ago, The Commentary was written by many Confucian scholars in the last period of Warring States (475 B.C.– 221 B.C.). Thus, there is a five-hundred to six-hundred-year period between these two books. Through thousands of years of peoples' experiences of studying and using the books, including the work of innumerable scholars, no contradiction was found between the contexts of the I Ching as a text of both divination *and* philosophy. So, because the interpretation of the texts of the I Ching had been greatly influenced by Confucian scholars' philosophical minds, divination became a tool for guiding people to pursue auspicious occasions and avoid ill fortune.

Since the texts of the I Ching direct people to act according to their situation and its timing 天时地利, people do not consider I Ching merely a book of divination, but also a guiding book to rectify their behavior.

The Commentary, which is supported by the philosophy of the yin and the yang, says:

> *One yin and one yang, this is the Tao.*
> *As a sustainer, it is excellent.*
> *As an accomplisher, it shows his nature.*
> *The benevolent encounter it, calling it benevolence.*
> *The wise encounter it, calling it wisdom.*
> *People use it every day but are not aware of it . . .*

This statement is intended to expose the Tao of I, the principle that yin and yang alternate. Alternation between the yin and the yang is the Tao of Heaven, and also the Tao of I.

Most people think the yin and the yang are contrary, opposite and conflicting. Actually, opposites in contradiction is only one aspect of the yin and yang. The intention of I Ching stresses more the harmony, transformation and wax and wane of the yin and the yang, and this typical way of thinking of the I Ching became a characteristic way of thinking for the Chinese. Thus, the Commentary says that for those who are able to pursue this thinking, it is auspicious.

The Commentary mentions,

> *In ancient times the holy sages made the Book of I, their purpose was to comprehend the order of their nature and fate. Therefore, they established the Tao of Heaven and called it yin and yang. They determined the Tao of Earth and called it yielding and firm. They determined the Tao of man and called it benevolence and righteousness. They conceptualized these three*

fundamental Powers and doubled them, therefore, in the Book of I a symbol of six lines was formed and named The Accomplished Gua.

Westerners called the six-lined symbol a "hexagram" according to their nomenclature.

It is worth mentioning that Lao Zi, having been influenced by the I Ching, established Taoism, which emphasized the Tao of Heaven. Confucius having been influenced by the I Ching, established Confucianism, which emphasized the Tao of Humanity. I Ching is the only book that influenced both Lao Zi and Confucius.

The Master, Confucius, says in The Commentary:

Writing cannot express words wholly. Words cannot express thought wholly. Are we unable to understand the thoughts of holy sages?

And the Master himself responds,

The holy sages set up the images and symbols in order to express their thoughts wholly; they devised the six lines in order to express the true and false wholly, then they appended judgments so they could express their words wholly.

By means of the six lines – the hexagram – the Chinese, through thousands of years, became used to representing thoughts through symbols, which the *I* names "symbolic thinking 形象思维." Through "symbolic thinking 形象思维," the ancients invented pictographs and pictographic characters. In the minds of Chinese readers, the pictographic characters evoke imagery through which they immediately come to understand the meaning of the characters.

Once, Ji Lu 季路, one of the students of Confucius, asked about serving the spirits of the dead. The Master said, "While you are not able to serve man, how can you serve their spirit?"

At another time, Ji Lu said, "I venture to ask about death." The Master then said, "While you do not know life, how can you know about death?"

These statements fully make it clear that Confucius was not interested in spirit and death.

If not for elucidating these subjects, then, what *was* the Master's approach to studying I Ching? The Master says, "On studying I Ching, stop divining, that's all! 学易不占而已矣!" And Xun Zi 荀子 (313 – 238 B.C), another famous Confucian scholar in the period of Warring States, who bore the same attitude as Confucius upon studying the I Ching said, "Be good at *I*, then need not divination 善为易者不占!"

Thus, it can be seen that the most important contribution of The Commentary was transforming the interpretation of I Ching from that of witchcraft and superstition, to philosophy and rational knowledge.

The Two Schools

After the Han dynasty (206 B.C. – 220 A.D.), Iology, the branches of learning the I Ching, divided into two schools: the Morality and Reason School 礼义学派 and the Symbol and Number School 象数学派. In addition, there were six independent sects 六宗 that splintered off from the two primary schools. All of them considered I Ching as a book for helping people in making decisions and formulating strategies.

The Song dynasty (960 A.D. – 1279 A.D.) was a flourishing period of study of the I Ching. All schools devoted themselves to giving full play to the I Ching concepts of bringing peace and stability to the country, doing good for society and benefiting the people. Ouyang Xiu 欧阳修 (1007 A.D. – 1072 A.D.), a famous writer of the Northern Song dynasty, pointed out, "All Six Classics record the Way of saints but the I Ching particularly distinguishes the practice of the saints. Good luck or ill luck, success or failure, moving or keeping still, forward or retreat . . . are all matters of the I Ching."

Cheng Yi 程颐 (1033 A.D. – 1107 A.D.), a distinguished philosopher of the Northern Song dynasty observed, "All six lines of the I Ching are useful to everyone – saints have saints' uses, the virtuous have virtuous uses, the common people have common people's uses, the supreme ruler has supreme ruler's uses, officials have officials' uses . . . nothing is beyond the reach of the I Ching."

Yang Wan Li 杨万里 (1127 A.D. – 1206 A.D.), a famous poet of the Southern Song dynasty, went a step further, declaring:

> I Ching not only speaks about "changes" but also talks about "unobstructed changes 通变." "Change" concerns the changes of objective things or reality. "Unobstructed change 通变" is about one's subjective tactics of responding to the changes. During the changes of things or circumstances there is gain or loss, success or failure, peace or unrest . . . they are not always as one wishes and they are not under one's control. This is what the saint is concerned with. Only the way of "unobstructed change" is able to inspire people's wisdom and guide them to making proper decisions.

I of the Past Hundred Years

I consider myself so fortunate to have personally experienced a hundred-year cycle – from the suppression of Confucius and Confucianism, to a resurgence of high regard for Confucius and Confucianism once again. From the beginning of my study of the I Ching, I highly regarded the Ten Wings written by Confucius and his students, and considered it to be the finest reference. I held this opinion because Confucius was the one living closest in time to the birth of the I Ching – only about a 500-year interval. Nevertheless, since the May Fourth Movement in China, at the dawn of the last century in 1919, "the radicals" attempted to completely deny Confucius and Confucianism, as well as Chinese culture.

After the Communists took over China in 1949, a policy of class struggle was continuously applied for fifty years. I Ching was denounced as a book of feudalism and superstition, and was banished from the market.

Aiming to strangle ancient culture, in April 1957 the Communist Party plotted a movement called the "Letting a Hundred Flowers Bloom" campaign. Intellectuals were earnestly invited and strongly advised to contribute their opinions on national policy issues. Responding to the call, many condemned corruption and criticized the Party monopoly on political power. However, after only five weeks, the Party turned the "Letting a Hundred Flowers Bloom" campaign into an "Anti-Rightist" campaign. During this campaign, 300,000 to 600,000 intellectuals were labeled as rightist; their jobs were taken away and many were sent to labor camps. In the end, the Party tried to cover up the truth, quibbling that its tactics were "an overt conspiracy" that lured "the snakes out of their holes."

Eight years afterwards, in 1966, the "Cultural Revolution" was launched. This movement lasted for ten years, during which time a hundred-million people suffered from wandering about with no homes, and twenty-million died. In the meantime, the class struggle reached its summit, like the sun high at noon. But soon, after another thirty years, the Cultural Revolution was considered devilish and looked upon as filth to be ruthlessly thrown away like a pair of worn out shoes.

On the other hand, the fate of the I Ching – which gave birth to Chinese culture – has been remarkable. Gloriously, after 5,000 years of ups and downs, this book promoting morality, peace and harmony is shining over humanity brighter than ever, demonstrating that, "The true gold fears no fire 真金不怕火炼."

2

周 易 的 灵 魂
The Soul of the I Ching

Seeking Harmony

The soul of the I Ching is Seeking Harmony.

The oldest document preserved in China is The Book of History 书经. Its first piece of writing is The Canon of Yao 尧典. It is a proclamation issued by King Yao 尧帝, the chief of a tribe-commune in ancient China 3,000 years ago. It says:

> 克明俊德, 以亲九族. 九族既睦, 平章百姓. 百姓昭明, 协和万邦.
> *Select a virtuous and able person to be the chief and train him to seek harmony with nine clans.*
> *After nine clans get along well, then handle the affairs of a hundred different surname families.*
> *After the affairs of a hundred different surname families have been well managed, then seek harmony with ten thousand nations.*

In those days, people of the same blood relationship of nine generations lived together forming a clan-commune. The clan-commune was a sub-unit of a country. Every clan-commune selected a virtuous and able person to manage the affairs of the commune. The primary mission of the chief was to unite the members of nine clans. "Nine clans" indicates nine generations living together in a clan-commune – four generations up and four generations down plus the fundamental household. Once the members of nine clans are getting along well, then a hundred different surname families will be well managed. After hundreds of different surname families are well managed, then harmony can be sought with ten thousand nations.

When King Yao was in power, the chiefs of all the tribe communes recommended Shun 舜 to be King Yao's successor. King Yao went through a three-year period of testing the integrity of Shun 舜, who proved to be virtuous and able. Eventually, King Yao abdicated his position and handed it to Shun.

After Shun took on his responsibilities, he went a step further making a still dignified request to the people known as the "Five Norms 五教": that the father should be just, the mother should be loving, the elder brother should be friendly, the younger brothers should be respectful, and the sons should be devoted to the family's best interests. Beginning with Shun, the Five Norms have been traditionally practiced for over 4,000 years by most Chinese families until the Communists took over China.

During the time of the Xia, the Shang and the Zhou – referred to as the "three dynasties" 三代 – China had already expanded to become a large country. A principle to rule the country had been instituted, known as "Hong Fan 洪范," which is similar to a constitution of nowadays.

Hong 洪 means "the greatest" and Fan 范 "the norm," and this principle became the standard for the administration of the country. The spirit of the norm was known as "wang tao 王道," which stipulated that there should be "no clique nor partiality in the country 无党无偏," and that "the government should be benevolent, fair and just 王道平平."

While Hong Fan was concerned with the internal policy of the country, another proclamation issued by King Yao addressed external policy, and this too has also been preserved in The Canon of Yao 尧典. It says, "先王耀德不观兵. The ancient kings illuminated virtues and never made shows of strength."

At one point, King Mu of Zhou 周穆王 intended to send armed forces to suppress 犬戎 Quan Rong, a strong opponent of Zhou, on its western border. A minister of King Mu reaffirmed King Yao's proclamation to admonish King Mu that it was a long-held tradition of earlier kings to never commit aggression against neighboring kingdoms 侵略, nor to seek out hegemony 称霸.

*   *   *

Seeking Harmony, which is a matter of course to the Chinese, has been practiced for 5,000 years and is clearly recorded in the I Ching.

The Commentary on the Decision of the first gua, Initiating 乾 ☰, says,

乾道变化, 各正性命. 保合太和, 乃利贞. 首出庶物, 万国咸宁.

The way of Initiating works through change and transformation, so that each being receives its true nature and destiny and comes to protect and defend the Supreme Harmony jointly – this is what furthers and what preserves. Towering high above the multitude of things it furthers the tranquility and peace of all nations.

Grandpa's Instruction

My first mentor in the study of the I Ching was my Grandpa. I still remember how he emphasized to me that the soul of the I Ching is: "Defending and protecting the Supreme Harmony jointly furthers the tranquility and peace of all nations."

I remember well in the spring of 1937, when I was sixteen, Grandpa brought me to Peking for a vacation to celebrate my coming into manhood. First we visited the Imperial Palace 故宫. After we passed through the gate, Grandpa found a tea stall under some shade trees on the right. He said, "We will be here a whole day long. It's wise to take a little break here." Grandpa ordered a pot of oolong tea. Then we sat down and he began his storytelling.

Grandpa said, "Today my major purpose is to show you the soul of the I Ching, which is fully demonstrated in the layout and the architecture here in the palace. First of all, the Imperial Palace is located in the center of Peking. It was the palace and residence of twenty-four emperors and the families of the Ming 明 and the Qing 清 dynasties. It took fourteen years to build beginning with the fourth emperor of the Ming dynasty, Emperor Yong Le 永乐大帝, in 1406, and it was completed in 1420."

As we were on our way to the buildings, Grandpa continued, "The palace was divided into two parts: the outer court 外朝 and the inner court 后宫. The outer court was used for ceremonial purposes and the inner court was the emperor's residential area."

After we went through the Gate of the Palace of Supreme Harmony 太和殿, Grandpa said, "Here is the outer court where the three major palaces 三大殿– the Palace of Supreme Harmony 太和殿, the Palace of Central Harmony 中和殿, and the Palace of Preserving Harmony 保和殿 – are situated. The three palaces were built along the central axis from south to north. The tallest and largest one in the front is the Palace of Supreme Harmony 太和殿. It signifies the soul of the Chinese culture, thus it is situated in the center of the cross-section of the palace, and indicates that, from time immemorial, the Chinese treasured harmony. It was not the commonly known harmony, but instead the Supreme Harmony, which denotes the highest harmony – the harmony between human and nature, the harmony between neighborhoods, the harmony amongst family, and the harmony amid all nations."

Grandpa continued to explain, "The guidebook says that the palace rises ninety-eight feet above the level of the surrounding square and that it is the tallest building in the Imperial Palace and is even the tallest building in Peking . . . It was the ceremonial center of imperial power . . . and it is nine bays wide and five bays deep . . ."

Grandpa asked me, "Do you know why it is nine bays by five bays?"

I answered, "I guess it must be to coincide with what the I Ching says regarding 'the venerability of Nine-Fifth 九五之尊.' That is, 'the yang element at the fifth place of a hexagram being regarded as the place belonging to the emperor.' It is a super auspicious place known as 'dragon flying in the sky' 飞龙在天 in the first gua, Initiating."

Behind the Palace of Supreme Harmony 太和殿, there are two palaces. The larger one at the rear is the Palace of Preserving Harmony 保和殿 and the smaller, which is only one-fourth as big as the Palace of Supreme Harmony, is in the middle. It is the Palace of Central Harmony 中和殿.

"Did you notice the square building in the middle?" Grandpa asked me.

I said, "Yes."

Grandpa went on, asking, "What is its name?"

"Palace of Central Harmony 中和殿," I responded.

Grandpa asked, "Why is this the only one amongst all the palaces that is square?"

What a tough question, I thought! Then, I asked, "Grandpa, do you mind letting me think for a while?" Grandpa nodded his head with a smile.

As I walked around the square building I thought, the shape must be related to the word "central 中". Then a thought flashed into my mind that in the I Ching the central position is always highly esteemed 尚中. The Commentary says, "The second place of the hexagram gets praise regularly 二多誉 and the merit of the fifth place is often noted 五多功 because both of them are in central places." Also, in Chinese minds, the concepts of "central" and "square" are always related to being righteous and upright, as the Chinese have always said "central-righteousness 中正 and squarely upright 方正."

When we were little, teachers reminded us that, in writing, we should always make the characters square 方 and upright 正. The meaning of the second line of the sixteenth gua Delight is, "Erect as firmly as rock not merely for a whole day . . . It is central and upright."

When I proudly reported my "discovery" to Grandpa, I expected high praise . . . but he said nothing, and only nodded and gently stroked my head.

"Central Harmony 中和, in Chinese, bears the meaning of neutral, impartial, without leaning to the left nor to the right. It is the harmony of the yin and the yang mutually coordinated with each other," he said at last.

Then, we were in front of the Palace of Preserving Harmony 保和殿. Grandpa said, "Think about the meaning of the name, the Palace of Preserving

Harmony 保和殿. It reminds people how essential *harmony* is! – Where there is harmony, preserve it and protect it. Where there is no harmony, create it. Where there is not enough harmony, replenish it." And then he added, "Just imagine if there is no harmony, what would happen to our life? When the Mongolians took over China, people were divided into four classes: the Mongolians 蒙古人, the Semu 色目人, the Hans 汉人, and the Southerners 南人. Since the Mongolian government practiced a policy of racial discrimination, there was no harmony. Thus they were only in power for ninety-nine years . . ."

After a short while, Grandpa spoke again: "In 1644, after the Manchu nation 满族 took over China, the Imperial Court divided into two political groups: the moderates and the hardliners. The hardliners stood for massacre. With the intention of seeking peace and stability, they adopted a policy of 'executing one as a warning to a hundred' and slaughtered a great number of those who opposed them. But their experiences demonstrated to them that it wouldn't do any good. On the contrary, it made things even worse. At last, they changed their attitude and adopted a policy of 'Harmony, yet not alike 和而不同.' Thus, this policy laid the foundation for its two-hundred-year rule."

After thinking for a while, Grandpa said, "When Emperor Kang Xi 康熙 (1654 – 1772) compiled the book, Zhou I – The Code of Conduct 周易折中, he wrote the Preface himself, stating: 'I, as an emperor, rely upon Zhou I. In light of Zhou I, I began my national reconstruction. I began to study Zhou I when I was a boy. Now, I am over fifty and soon will be sixty. I deeply feel how important this book is to our country and its politics.' "

As we went through the Gate of the Inner Court 后宫, we saw another set of three palaces. The largest in front was the Palace of Heavenly Purity 乾清宫. In the middle was the smallest, the Hall of Union 交泰殿. In the rear was a medium-sized one, the Palace of Earthly Tranquility 坤宁宫.

Grandpa remarked, "How beautiful the meanings of those names are! We should look upon the design and reflect on the comprehensive meanings of the names given to these buildings."

While we were walking about he continued, "Think about the Palace of Heavenly Purity 乾清宫 being in the front and the Palace of Earthly

Tranquility 坤宁宫 being situated at the rear. Is it Heaven matching Earth and Heaven's purity matching Earth's tranquility? When heaven is pure, it is warm and sunny, a bright sun with a gentle breeze. Then, people on earth enjoy tranquility and peacefulness. It is most significant that the Hall of Union 交泰殿 is in the middle. The names of the palaces demonstrate what the I Ching says,

> Heaven and Earth unite, all beings come into union.
> The upper and the lower link; their wills are the same.

And The Commentary on the Symbol says,

> *Heaven and Earth are moving together. The ruler gives full play to his ability and wisdom to complete the Tao of Heaven and the Tao of Earth and assist their suitable arrangement to influence people.*

Grandpa spoke again: "Heaven and Earth uniting is actually the yin and the yang uniting. Or more specifically, it is their energies that unite. Tai 泰 is one of the most auspicious words in the Chinese language. Originally it meant 'more than' or 'most.' It generally indicates a condition of being more than great. Tai 泰 also means peace, safety, security, good health; or it suggests progression, proceeding and advancement. I think the English translation 'union' only expresses half of the meaning. Actually, in Chinese, the name of the palace contains the twofold meaning of 'union 交' and 'to advance 泰.' I think it is best translated as 'the Palace of Advancing Union 交泰殿.'"

While we were talking, we had unwittingly already entered the Imperial Garden. It was small and compact, containing several elaborate landscaped areas. Grandpa told me, "Beginning from the Han dynasty (206 B.C. – 220 A.D.), the I Ching was respected as a *classic* recommended to all scholars for serious study. After it had been assigned as the required reference for attending the Imperial Examination from the Han dynasty until the Qing dynasty (1644 A.D. – 1911 A.D.), 3,000 to 4,000 books related to the study of the I Ching and Iology appeared."

For me, time went by too fast, and the sun had already set be western hills. Grandpa was afraid I would get too tired and suggesteu ɩnat we should leave. "If we are still interested in Imperial Palace, we can always come again," he said.

On the way back to the hotel, secretly I was proud of Grandpa. How fortunate I was to have such a learned Grandpa and to receive such a unique gift to celebrate my coming of age — a gift that would influence my whole life.

Quite surprisingly, fifty years later, the seed Grandpa had planted deep in my heart suddenly sprouted. When I worked on *The Complete I Ching* in the 1980s, at one point, when I was translating the thirteenth gua, Tong Ren 同人 ䷌, regarded the image, and read the Decision and The Commentary of the Decision, I experienced a compulsion to translate the name of the Tong Ren 同人 as Seeking Harmony.

The Decision of the gua is 同人于野 Seeking Harmony amongst people. The Commentary on the Decision says: 柔得位得中而应乎乾. 文明以健, 中正而应, 君子正也. 唯君子能通天下之志. Translated into English, it says,

> *The yielding obtains the proper place. It is central. It corresponds with Qian, the Initiating, implying brilliance with strength, central and corresponding. This is the correct way for the superior person. Only the superior person is able to convey the wills of all under Heaven.*

Immediately I recalled the scenes of the Imperial Palace and all the stories Grandpa had told me, especially about both the soul of the I Ching and the soul of Chinese culture . . . All these were vividly reflected in the layout and the names on the major palaces – the Palace of Supreme Harmony, the Palace of Central Harmony, the Palace of Preserving Harmony,–the Palace of Heavenly Purity, the Palace of Earthly Tranquility, and the Palace of the Advancing Union . . . I comprehend now deeply that the name of the gua should be Seeking Harmony.

On the eve of the twentieth century in 1999, the International Biographical Centre in Cambridge, England, selected me as one of five-hundred people around the world to write an essay for The Millennium Time Capsule, which would be buried in 2000 and then exhumed and displayed for the guidance of the people of the third millennium. In this essay, I wrote:

> Deep in my heart I always hold faith in the future.
>
> I believe with confidence that the twenty-first century will be a century of seeking harmony and great harvest.[2] Through seeking harmony, prosperity and affluence will be harvested in all nations. And eventually, international harmony and world peace will at last be reaped in the third millennium.
>
> Furthermore, I believe firmly, that humanity is evolving to a higher level. After the physical and mental aspects of human evolution have reached a certain point, an evolution of the spiritual aspect will play a dominant role. According to the I Ching, after seeking harmony we will obtain a great harvest. After the great harvest, we will be most humble. And after being most humble we will be able to enjoy great delight. This is the spiritual journey of the whole of humanity.

---

2 Seeking Harmony is the thirteenth gua. Following this gua in sequence are Great Harvest, Humbleness and Delight.

3

周 易 的 体 系
The System of the I Ching

Since ancient times, as we noted in Chapter 1, there were two schools of study of the I Ching – one, the School of Morality and Reason 理义; the other, the School of Symbols and Numbers 象数. The School of Morality and Reason emphasizes the significance of the text and its moral messages. The Symbols and Numbers School stresses the symbols and their inherent numerology and the lines of the hexagrams and their relationships with each other.

This book, *Understanding the I Ching,* is for laypersons; thus it is concerned with both aspects.

Moral reasoning is inseparable from the symbols and their associated numerology. Symbols and numbers corresponding to the gua are as shadows cast by illuminated physical objects. Through observing the myriad phenomena of the universe, the ancients created the gua. By examining the relationships between the lines of the gua and their symbolic meanings, the ancients were able to explain the changes in those phenomena. Thus, to understand the I Ching, one should first become familiar with the symbolic meanings of the gua.

Besides, I Ching was a book of symbols long before it became a book of written language. At the beginning, it existed in the form of symbols only, and symbols are still the key to a true understanding of the I Ching.

Symbols in I Ching are represented by gua 卦. Most English versions translate gua as "trigram" or "hexagram" depending on the context. In Chinese, gua 卦 means "hanging up 褂." That is, hanging up the symbols of the gua for people to see, so they know how to act to manifest good fortune and to avoid misfortune. There are eight trigrams, which are combined in pairs to create sixty-four hexagrams. Thus, to learn the rudiments of the I Ching, one has first to recognize the eight trigrams and become familiar with their forms, names, natures and significances.

Eight Trigrams

Regarding the eight trigrams there is an ancient rhyme which says:

Heaven and Earth determine the direction,	天地定位
Forces of Mountain and Lake are united.	山泽通气
Thunder and Wind arouse each other,	雷风相薄
Water and Fire combat one another.	水火相射

This rhyme fully reveals the yin-yang philosophy of the I Ching. Eight trigrams represent eight fundamental substances in the universe. Traditionally they are split into four yin and yang pairs:

Heaven ☰ and Earth ☷, Water ☵ and Fire ☲
Thunder ☳ and Wind ☴, Mountain ☶ and Lake ☱

The nature of the elements in each pair are opposite to each other; at the same time they are mutually dependent upon one another. Just imagine, if there were only Heaven without Earth or only Earth without Heaven, what kind of universe would it be? Regarding Fire and Water, usually we say, "They are as incompatible as fire and water," to describe the antagonism between the two conflicting elements. However, in our daily lives, fire and water work together jointly to benefit our lives.

The names of the gua are the names of the symbols. Concomitant with being a student of the I Ching, one is required to be familiar with the names of the gua and able to associate them with the symbols they represent, their attributes and meanings. An ancient verse has been handed down for the convenience of students in recognizing and memorizing the eight trigrams.

Qian, the initiating Heaven, has three solid lines.　　　　☰

Kun, the responding Earth, has three broken lines.　　　　☷

Zhen, the arousing Thunder, is like a cup standing upright.　☳

Xun, the penetrating Wind, has a crack in its bottom.　　　☴

Kan, the dangerous *Water*, is firm in the center.　　　　☵

Li, the clinging Fire, is disconnected in the middle.　　　☲

Gen, the stable Mountain, is like a bowl lying face down.　☶

Dui, the joyous Lake, has an opening on the top.　　　　☱

This idea of "unity of opposites 对立统一" was not a coincidence but instead an intentional arrangement, revealing the essential wisdom of the ancients and its plain description. It was an embryonic form of the saying, "One yin and one yang is what the Tao says 一阴一阳谓之道."

Heaven ☰, Thunder ☳, Water ☵ and Mountain ☶ are yang gua. Earth ☷, Wind ☴, Fire ☲ and Lake ☱ are yin gua. In order to distinguish yin and yang gua, we apply some simple rules:

- If all lines are yin lines, then it is a yin gua.
- If all lines are yang lines, then it is a yang gua.
- In accordance with the principle of "the one leads the many," if there is only one yin line, it is a yin gua.
- If there is only one yang line, it is a yang gua.

These trigrams are significant. They are the basic components forming the sixty-four hexagrams. Two trigrams combined – with one above and the other below – constitute a hexagram. Recognizing the images of the trigrams and understanding their significance greatly helps one to understand the contexts of the sixty-four hexagrams.

Three Powers 三才

Of all the elements in the universe, the ancients regarded three elements as most significant – Heaven, Earth and Humanity. Heaven is on the top, Earth is at the bottom and Humanity is in the middle. Humanity is the bridge between Heaven and Earth. This understanding is the root of King Wen's philosophy and the central theme of *Zhou I* – *the unity of Heaven and Humanity* 天人合一. Thus, in a six-lined gua (the hexagram), the two top positions represent Heaven, the two bottom positions represent Earth, and the two middle positions represent Humanity.

The yin-yang philosophy of the I Ching is expressed by means of a well-organized system of symbols and associated numerology. It is a combination of the forms of symbols and their numerology, as well as the context of morality and reason. For instance, the bottom line of the first gua Initiating represents "dragon lying low," and the second line represents "dragon becoming visible in the field," because they are in the Earth portions. The third and fourth lines are related to the superior person – the third line represents: "All day long, initiating, initiating . . ." and the fourth line represents: "Dragon chooses either leaping out of or resting in the abyss." Then the fifth line represents "dragon flying in the sky," and the top line represents "dragon becoming haughty," because the dragon is rising high in the sky.

Two Phases 两体

Every six-lined gua, a hexagram, is made up of two three-lined gua, the trigrams. There is a lower gua and an upper gua. The lower gua is also called the inner gua and the upper gua is also called the outer gua. Together, they reveal the inner spirit and the outer expression of the gua.

As every gua represents a phenomenon, thus every gua has an essence and a form. In order to understand a phenomenon, one should understand both its form as well as its essence. In order to understand a gua, one has to understand its inner and outer situations as well as its inner spirit and outer expressions.

Generally, the inner gua represents one's subjective motivation for development and growth; the outer gua represents the objective situation in which one develops and grows. One's inner motivation can affect one's outer situation; conversely, one's outer situation can affect one's inner motivation. If the inner motivation is strong, its effect upon the outer situation will be great. But, if the effect of the inner motivation upon the outer situation is too great, then the inner motivation will be diminished. Thus, in understanding a gua or dealing with a situation, one has to pay attention to both the inner and the outer gua components.

The third and the fourth lines in a hexagram constitute the human lines. The human lines are positioned between the Heaven above and the Earth below. The human lines can ascend upward or descend downward. They can advance or retreat. When the human line ascends, it can be healthy and wealthy, wise and spiritual. It has the potential to become a sage. Thus, the ancient sages paid attention to educating others and to self-cultivation. When the human line descends, it can be unhealthy and insignificant, unwise and unspiritual. It can become mean. This is human nature. Thus, in most cases, the third line tends to be unfavorable; the fourth line tends to be worried and apprehensive.

Seating Arrangement 位次

The "Three Powers" (Heaven, Earth, Humanity) are expressed with the lower, middle and upper pairs of lines in a hexagram. The ancients created a system known as the "seating arrangement 位次." To distinguish the position of the six lines, the ancients titled the first line on the bottom the "initial place." And successively titled the second line from the bottom the "second place," the third line from the bottom the "third place" . . . up to the sixth line at the top the "top place."

To embody the yin-yang philosophy, the ancients assigned the initial place the "yang place," the second place the "yin place," the third place the "yang place," the fourth place the "yin place," the fifth place the "yang place," and the top place the "yin place." Therefore, the initial place is the place of "the yang place in the Earth portion"; the second place is "the yin place in the Earth portion." The third place is "the yang place in the Human portion"; the fourth place is "the yin place in the human portion." The fifth place is "the yang place in the Heaven portion," and the top place is "the yin place in the Heaven portion."

Amongst the sixty-four gua, only the gua prior to the last gua, Already Fulfilled ䷾, is in complete alignment with these rules of seating arrangement stated above. The appearance of this gua manifests all firm elements located in the yang places and all yielding elements located in the yin places. Since all elements get their proper places, the gua bears the name "Already Fulfilled." The symbolic and numeric forms of the six lines of the hexagram are in accord with the moral and reasoning context of the yin-yang philosophy. Therefore, each of the sixty-four hexagrams becomes an integral part of the unity of Heaven, Earth and Humanity.

Functions of the Lines

As lines make up the gua, therefore the attribute of a gua is determined by the attributes of the lines and by their combinations, arrangements and interrelationships.

Modern science suggests that different combinations and arrangements of elements produce molecules of different chemical substances. This principle can be applied to human affairs. In human society, different combinations of people with different attributes – yin or yang personalities – in a group, determine the characteristics of the overall group. If each member of a group of three people alternates as a leader, three different styles of leadership will appear. Consequently, the group will function in three different ways.

The combinations and arrangements of the six lines become intricate and complex when related to the sixty-four gua. In order to determine the attributes of the gua, one has to consider the complicated relationships of the yin and the yang lines as well as their sequence.

Sequence of the Lines

The sequence of the lines begins from the bottom. The ancients held that everything started at the bottom. Thus, the first, or the lowest, line is called the "initial line." The second lowest is called the "second line." The third lowest is called the "third line," and so on. The sixth line is called the "top line."

The Name of the Line

Lines are differentiated into yin and yang lines. The ancients nicknamed yang lines "Nine," because Nine is the greatest among the five odd numbers 1, 3, 5, 7, 9, and it is yang's nature to lead. They nicknamed yin lines "Six," because Six is in the central among the five even numbers 2, 4, 6, 8, 10, and it is yin's nature to hold the center. Thus, a second yang line would be named "Second Nine," while a sixth yin line would be named "Top Six."

Getting the Place 得位 and Losing the Place 失位

Amongst the sixty-four gua, except for Already Fulfilled, each of the rest of the sixty-three gua has the problem of the yin and the yang not being in the proper place. So the ancients established the rule of "getting the place" and "losing the place." "Getting the place" indicates that the yang element is in the yang place and the yin element is in the yin place. If not, either the yang element or the yin element is "losing the place."

Carrying 承, Mounting 乘, Neighboring 比 and Corresponding 应

Owing to the constant flowing of matters and things, there are no unalterable, static patterns. The yin-yang elements, which reflect the flowing of these matters and things, are constantly changing positions. In order to reflect these intricate and complicated conditions, the ancients created the rules of "carrying," "mounting," "neighboring" and "corresponding."

Carrying 承 and Mounting 乘

Within a pair of two lines, contrast the upper one with the lower one. The lower one is said to be carrying the upper one; and the upper one is said to be the lower one. If a yang line mounts on a yin line, the yang governing the yin, it is auspicious. On the other hand, when a yang line is carrying a yin line, the yang line is controlled by the yin line, which portends misfortune.

Neighboring 比 and Holding Together 相比

Each pair of lines stand side by side, forming a neighboring relationship. The initial and the second, the second and the third, the fourth and the fifth, and the fifth and the top are neighboring pairs. How about the third and the fourth lines? Because they are in positions between the inner gua and the outer gua, they cannot form a neighboring relationship.

In forming a neighboring relationship, the elements of the pair should be one yin and the other yang. If the two elements are both yang or both yin, they cannot be neighboring pairs. The neighboring relationship is actually the same as carrying and mounting, only the yin-yang nature of the elements should be seen in the context of this specific condition.

Responding 应, Corresponding 相应, Anti-responding 敌应

Every hexagram is made up of two trigrams. The first three lines make up the lower trigram and the next three lines make up the upper trigram. The first line of the lower trigram responds to the first line of the upper trigram, the second line of the lower trigram responds to the second line of the upper trigram, and the third line of the lower trigram responds to the third line of the upper trigram. In other words, the initial line responds to the fourth line, the second line responds to the fifth line and the third line responds to the top line. Between any two responding lines, if one is yin and the other is yang, they are corresponding to each other 相应. If these two lines are both yin or both yang, they are anti-responding to each other. For instance, in Advance ䷊ (11), all responding lines are corresponding to each other 相应. In Initiating ䷀ (1), all responding lines are anti-responding to each other 敌应. In the case of two responding lines corresponding to each other, the yin and yang coordinate and cooperate. It is possible that the initial line and the fourth line, the second line and the fifth line, and the third line and the top line are all corresponding to each other. This situation occurs in Already Fulfilled☷☵ (63) and Not Yet Fulfilled ☲☵ (64).

Amongst the sixty-four hexagrams, there is only one situation, Already Fulfilled ☷☵ (63), in which all responding lines correspond with each other and all six lines are "getting the places." In contrast, there is a situation with the gua Not Yet Fulfilled ☲☵ (64) in which all responding lines are corresponding with each other but all six lines are "losing the place."

These rules related to symbols and their associated numerology reveal the unity of Heaven, Earth and Humanity, which on one hand emphasizes the differentiation of the firm and the yielding, and on the other hand stresses the unity of the yin and the yang. The harmony of Heaven, Earth and Humanity is achieved through their unity 辩证统一, their separation 分 or linking 合.

With regard to the separation of the firm and the yielding, the dominance of the firm and the subordination of the yielding should not be neglected. Yang should be leading, taking the initiative; yin should be subordinate and following. Yang should rely on yin giving full play to its lead and yin should yield to yang to cooperate and assist. This kind of leading and following relationship should not be turned upside down. But, owing to the interdependency of yin and yang, they should be complementary to each other, and the hard and the yielding should coordinate and harmonize. *Zhou I* is based upon this integral harmony as a whole to establish these rules.

Time, Timing, Time-Situation 时义

The six lines of each hexagram are subject to the rules of "carrying," "mounting," "neighboring" and "responding," which together form the essential nature 主旨, which the ancients named "the significance of the gua 卦义." In Chinese, it is called "the significance of the time 时义." Many scholars just call it "time 时."

However, personally, I would like to call it "time-situation" – which means the specific timing in the specific situation. Most Chinese believe that to be successful one should seize three things: the proper timing 天时, the favorable situation 地利 and the harmonious relationship 人和. Among these three, the critical one is harmonious relationship. Therefore, in accordance with my understanding, what every hexagram represents is the specific "time-situation" for one to follow or to avoid. For example, the Commentary for the third line of the third hexagram, Beginning ䷂, "Chasing deer, no guide, in the midst of woods. The superior person is alert. Give up! Going forward: humiliation."

Harmonious and Disharmonious Situation

The "timing" or "timing-situation" of the sixty-four hexagrams represent the sixty-four "phases of time." They are sixty-four models of the natural or social changings in different conditions – either the harmonious or disharmonious conditions.

Usually in harmonious situations:

> There is coordination of the yin and the yang 阴阳协调.
> There is mutual cooperation of the firm and the yielding 刚柔并济.
> There is moving forward jointly from both the yin and the yang sides 双向互动.
> There is cooperation from coordination of both the firm and the yielding 协同 配合.

In disharmonious situations:

> There is the firm occupying the supreme place, but it does not communicate with the yielding; like Hindrance ䷋ (12).
> The yang element develops too fast, which makes the yin to prosper and the yang to decline; like Great Exceeding ䷛ (28).
> There is too much yielding, which destroys the yin-yang balance; like Exhausting ䷮ (47).
> The contradiction of yin and yang becomes an un-reconciled condition; like Abolishing the Old ䷰ (49).

Yang Encounters Yin / Yin Encounters Yang

"When the yang element encounters the yin element, there is no block. When the yang element encounters the yang element, there is no way going forward."

These two rules are handed down from Master Shang Bing-He (1870 -1950), an eminent I Ching scholar at the end of the last century. By examining the two yang elements on the bottom of the twenty-sixth gua, Great Accumulation ䷙, one can see that they are blocked, yet the third yang element is able to go through without obstruction. The structure of the hexagram is Mountain above and Heaven below. The attribute of Heaven is active; it tends to move forward. The Yao Text of the bottom line, Initial Nine, says, "There is adversity. Favorable to stop advancing." This is because the second line is a yang element. Then, The Yao Text of the second line says, "A wagon's axle bracket comes off." What is actually meant by this is: "There is no way to go forward." This is because the third line is a yang element too. Then, what is the situation with the third yang line? The Yao Text says, "A good horse chases. Favorable to be steadfast and upright in hardship. Practice charioteering and defense daily. Favorable to have somewhere to go." Why is the situation of the third yang line "favorable to have somewhere to go"? The reason is that the fourth line is a yin element! The rule Master Shang handed down says, "When yang element encounters yang element, there is no way going forward."

Centrality 中, Central Harmony 中和, Central Unbiased 中正

For expressing the best integration of the yin and the yang, the ancients created the rule of "centrality 中." It is a kind of time-situation as well as a moral quality, which produces critical effects among the six lines. For instance, every line located in the middle of either the upper gua or the lower gua is considered "central." Each yang element staying at the central position is considered as bearing the virtue of "firm centrality 刚中"; it is firm, but fair and unbiased. Each yin element staying at the central position is considered to bear the virtue of "yielding central 柔中"; it is the yielding, but fair and unbiased. According to the I Ching, the second place is the place for the minister and the fifth place is the place for the king. In this case, the "central firm" corresponds with the "central yielding." It reflects that the king and the minister are working together with one accord and coordinating by tacit agreement. This is the best condition, with the yin and the yang fully integrated. The ancients called this condition "central harmony 中和." In case of the yin element situated in the second place and the yang element situated in the fifth place, this is both central and correct. In Chinese, this is called "central unbiased 中正."

In comparing central harmony 中和 with central unbiased 中正, which is better? Centrality is better than honesty, uprightness, fair-mindedness and unbiasedness. This is because unbiased is not necessarily central, yet being central will be unbiased without exception. In I Ching, if all six lines are getting the places, this is not necessarily auspicious; yet if both the second line and the fifth are getting the central places, most of them will be good luck. Therefore, *Zhou I* esteems centrality.

The Essence of Zhou I

The Master, Confucius, says in The Great Treatise: "The Initiating and the Responding are indeed the gateway to the *I*."

In The Commentary on the Symbol of the first gua, Initating, the Master says,

> *Heaven acts with vitality and persistence.*
> *In correspondence with this,*
> *The superior person keeps himself vital without ceasing.*

In The Commentary on the Symbol of the second gua, Responding, the Master says,

> *Earth's nature is responding and corresponding.*
> *In correspondence with this,*
> *The superior person enriches his virtue to sustain all beings.*

It is obvious then, that the purpose of the I Ching is to influence human beings to be superior persons. In doing so, they will keep themselves vital without ceasing and enrich their virtue to sustain all beings.

4

周易的卦主
The Host of the Gua

Each of the sixty-four gua represents a "time-situation" – in Chinese, chu jing 处境 – which articulates how one is to act properly at this time in this situation.

To understand the "time-situation" or the theme of the gua, one should grasp the significance of the "*host*" of the gua. The *host* reflects the essence of the gua. Some scholars name it the "*ruling line,*" because the *ruling line* discloses the gua's central theme. Without familiarity with the host of the gua, it is like a blind person coming in contact with an elephant only by touch; perplexed with regards to what he has encountered, he might lose his bearings and get lost. This might be one of the reasons that most people feel confused upon studying the I Ching. On the other hand, if the host is identified and its significance grasped, it is like having the key to unlock the door to the I Ching.

The time-situation of each gua is revealed in the Decision of the gua. It is believed that King Wen composed the Decisions. *Decision* in Chinese is tuan 彖 – also the name of a fierce animal with sharp teeth, for cutting. So the ancients employed this image to describe Decision – to imply judging, deciding and summarizing. As far as possible, they wanted rich content expressed in a succinct style to summarize each gua.

According to my experience, to determine the *host* it is best to examine the symbol in conjunction with the text of the Decision. As Master Shang Bing-he 尚秉和 (1870 – 1950) says, "There are no words attached to the gua without considering what the symbol reveals 无象外之辞."

Based upon the principle of "one rules many," generally one of the six lines will be the host; sometimes two. In most cases, the *host* locates at the second or the fifth place, because these two places are central. The fifth place is superior to the second, so the fifth place appears as a host more often.

For instance, the host of Initiating ☰ (1) is the yang element at the fifth place. It represents a flying dragon in the sky. It possesses the four virtues of being firm, vital, central and correct. It inherits the pure yang energy from Heaven. Thus the fifth line is the most appropriate line to be the host.

The host of Responding ☷ (2) is the yin element at the second place. It represents the Earth, a symbol of "straight, square and great." It possesses the four virtues of being yielding, submissive, central and correct, and inherits the pure yin energy from Earth. It too deserves the position of a host.

In some situations, a yin element at the fifth place can be the host; although it is not correct, it is central. It represents the central theme of the gua. For instance, the host of Great Harvest ䷍ (14) is a yin element at the fifth place, surrounded by five yang elements. In this time-situation, all five yang elements correspond to it, creating a great harvest condition. The Commentary on the Decision says, "The yielding obtains the honored position. Great and central. The upper and the lower correspond." Great Harvest is a well-known auspicious gua.

In certain circumstances, as previously mentioned, a gua has more than one host. For instance, the third gua, Beginning ䷂ (3). There are two yang elements, the firm at the initial place and the firm at the fifth place. Each of them is crucial to the theme of the gua; thus they share the role of the host.

Among the sixty-four gua, there are twelve gua in which the ratio of the yin and the yang elements is 1:5, or vise versa. If only one line is yin and the others are yang, the yin will be the *host* of the gua. On the other hand, if the one is yang and the others are yin, the yang will be the *host*. For instance, if there are five yang with one yin, as Little Accumulation ䷈ (9), Fulfillment

☷ (10), Seeking Harmony ☷ (13), Great Harvest ☷ (14), then the gua is a yin gua. Conversely, if there are five yin with one yang, as Multitude ☷ (7), Union ☷ (8), Humbleness ☷ (15), Delight ☷ (16), the gua is considered to be a yang gua.

The Commentary on the Decision of Union ☷ (8) says: "Due to its firmness and central position. The upper and the lower are corresponding." In this specific situation, the firm is at the unique place – the solid at the fifth place, central and correct. Examining the image of the gua, the upper gua of Union is Water ☵, and the lower gua is Earth ☷. The firm at the fifth place is in the exclusive condition, suitable to be the *host*. Take a look at the thirteenth gua, Seeking Harmony ☷ (13), The Commentary on the Decision says, "The yielding obtains the proper place. It is central and corresponds with Qian, the Initiating. This is Seeking Harmony." The image of the upper gua is Heaven ☰ and that of the lower gua is Fire ☲. The yin element is the only yin element in the gua, which situates in the center of the lower gua and corresponds with the yang element at the upper gua. Besides this line, there is no other choice for the *host*.

There are thirty gua in which the ratio of the yin and the yang elements is 4:2. If, among the six lines, the ratio of the yin and the yang is 4:2, choose which of the two is in a central place. If both of the lines are in the central place, then pick the one that is in the correct place to be the *host*. For instance, in Darkness ☵ (29), the yang element at the fifth place is the best choice for the host. For Brightness ☲ (30), the yin element at the second place is the first choice to be the host.

There are twenty gua in which the ratio of the yin and the yang is 3:3. In this case, select the one in the central place first. Then pick the one that is central and correct. For instance, in Exhausting ☱ (47), the two central places are occupied by yang lines. Then, consider which one is central and also correct. Therefore, the yang element at the fifth place should be the first choice to be the host.

The host or hosts of the gua are represented by a line or two lines of the gua. "Line," in Chinese, is yao 爻. Yao 爻 means "imitating." And in Chinese, their pronunciation is exactly the same, which reveals that the purpose of studying the I Ching is **to imitate** what the lines in the gua are doing.

Appropriate Usage of the I Ching

I still remember that, when I first visited Maui in 1990, someone introduced me to an "expert" of the I Ching, who consulted the I Ching every day for over twenty years and kept records. He told me that if one consulted the I Ching every day and kept records, these would show a certain unique pattern or patterns of the gua that frequently appeared to the one who consulted.

In July 2001, after *The International Feng Shui Conference* in Zurich, Switzerland, I accepted the invitation of two women to visit Ibiza, a small beautiful island belonging to Spain, for two weeks, to discuss the I Ching. To my surprise, I learned that each of them consulted the I Ching at least five times daily. When they had a dream, received a letter, or planned to visit a friend . . . they had to consult the I Ching.

I think all of these people bear a wrong attitude toward consulting the I Ching. Now, although even more Chinese I Ching scholars believe that I Ching is a book to teach people to deal with others or things appropriately, still, most people who consult the I Ching are expecting to get good fortune and avoid misfortune. What they fail to realize is that in order to get good fortune or avoid misfortune, one should behave properly. We just discussed the ruling line, the *host* of the gua, and the original meaning of gua – that is, to "imitate." As a student of the I Ching, *therefore,* one has to train himself to be "central," "correct" and "upright," "also corresponding with those who respond to us," and "act according to the 'time' and 'situation' . . ." This creates an internal reference to good conduct. Encountering a contentious situation without such an internal reference is like the famous story related by the Duke of Zhou of "chasing deer in the woods without a guide." It would be better to exit the situation than to persevere.

The Decision of the fifth gua, Needing, advises, "Be sincere and truthful!" Because truth is blocked, so he becomes extremely cautious, and stops the case at midpoint. And ends in good fortune.

* * *

The following is a list of the host or hosts of the sixty-four gua for reader's reference.

THE UPPER CANON

1. ☰ Initiating   Host: the firm at the fifth place

Initiating represents the yang energy in its purest form, the Tao of Heaven. The fifth place is the seat of Heaven. Initiating also represents the Tao of a leader, and the fifth place is the seat for a leader. One in this place inherits the pureness of the yang energy from Heaven and possesses the four virtues of being firm, vital, central and correct. The Commentary on Decision says, "As if mounting on six dragons soaring in the sky . . . the Initiating is high above all beings."

2. ☷ Responding   Host: the yielding at the second place

Responding represents the yin energy in its purest form, the Tao of Earth. The second place is the place of Earth. Responding also represents the Tao of a subordinate, and the second place is a seat for a subordinate. One in this place inherits the pureness of the yin energy from Earth and possesses the four virtues of being yielding, submissive, central and correct. The Commentary on the Decision says, "Predetermining; loses. Following; obtaining a master."

3. ䷂ Beginning   Host: the firm at the initial place
                                              the firm at the fifth place

Beginning possesses two yang elements: one on the bottom, the other at the fifth place. The firm on the bottom indicates the beginning. It commemorates the beginning of King Wen's establishment of the feudal lords as a means of rescuing people from the tyranny of the Shang dynasty.

The firm at the fifth place reflects that eventually King Wen was able to establish a magnanimous government, bringing peace and prosperity to the people.

4. ䷃ Childhood   Host: the firm at the second place
                                              the yielding at the fifth place

The Commentary on the Decision says, "It is not I who seeks the ignorant. The ignorant seek me. His will corresponds to mine." The firm at the second place represents the enlightener, central and firm. He is sympathetic to the ignorant and enlightens the child. The yielding at the fifth place represents the ignorant, who responds to the firm, and respects the enlightener; thus he is capable of receiving enlightenment

5. ䷄ Needing   Host: the firm at the fifth place

Humans need food to nourish the body and spirit. The firm at the fifth place is at the supreme position. The Commentary on the Decision says, "Needing: requiring faith and confidence to wait . . . being sincere and faithful. There will be great success . . . Being in the place assigned by Heaven; it is central and correct."

6. ䷅ Contention   Host: the firm at the fifth place

In a matter of contention, the firm at the fifth place represents an arbitrator. He is central and correct. The remaining five lines are the ones involved in the contention. The Commentary on the Decision says, "Favorable to see a great person; the central and correct is honored."

7. ䷆ Multitude   Host: the firm at the second place

The firm at the second place is the only yang element in this gua. Being the host of the multitude it is in a central place. The Commentary on the Decision says, "Firm and central, he obtains a response. Taking the risk of dangerous action, he confronts no hindrance. All people follow him, what mistake should there be?"

8. ䷇ Union   Host: the firm at the fifth place

The firm at the fifth place is the only yang element of the gua. It is central and correct, firm and strong. The Commentary on the Decision says, "Seeking union. Good fortune. It is for mutual help. The lower follow the upper . . . Due to its firmness and central position."

9. ䷈ Little Accumulation   Host: the yielding at the fourth place
                                                      the firm at the fifth place

The yielding at the fourth place is the only yin element of the gua. Although it is not central, it is correct. The Commentary on the Decision says, "The little obtains the ruling position. Those above and those below correspond to it. This is called Little Accumulation." The Commentary says again, "Strong and gentle, the firm is in the central place. In the end their will, will be fulfilled."

10. ☰ Fulfillment   Host: the yielding at the third place
                                              the firm at the fifth place

The Commentary on the Decision says, "Fulfill one's duty. The yielding treads upon the firm." The yin element at the third place resting on two yang elements gives the name of the gua: Fulfillment. In the midst of five yang elements, the situation is difficult. However, the firm at the fifth place is in a supreme position. The Commentary on the Decision says, "The firm is central and correct. Fulfill one's duty in the place of a ruler and feel no guilt. His brilliance shines."

11. ☷ Advance   Host: the firm at the second place
                                              the yielding at the fifth place

The theme of this gua is: the upper and the lower correspond and support each other bringing about a blissful situation. The Commentary on the Decision says, "The little is departing; the great is arriving . . . Heaven and Earth unite and all beings come into union. The upper and the lower link; their wills are the same." The firm at the second place is able to fulfill his duty as a subordinate to correspond and support the upper. And the yielding at the fifth place is able to fulfill his duty as the leader to coordinate and support the lower.

12. ☲ Hindrance   Host: the yielding at the second place
                                              the firm at the fifth place

The theme of the gua is: the upper and the lower do not correspond and support each other, resulting in misfortune. The Commentary on the Decision says, "The great is departing; the little is arriving. Heaven and Earth do not unite; all beings do not communicate. The upper and the lower do not link; there are no relations between states."

13. ䷌ Seeking Harmony   Host: the yielding at the second place
the firm at the fifth place

The yielding at the second place is the only yin element; it is seeking harmony with the five yang elements. The firm at the fifth place corresponds with the yielding at the second place, creating an auspicious situation. The Commentary on the Decision says, "The yielding obtains the proper place. It is central and corresponds with Qian ☰, the Initiating. This is Seeking Harmony.

14. ䷍ Great Harvest   Host: the yielding at the fifth place

The yielding at the fifth place is the only yin element of the gua. It lies in the supreme place and is humble, embracing all yang. The Commentary on the Decision says, "The yielding obtains the honored position, great and central. The upper and the lower respond, so the name of Great Harvest comes."

15. ䷎ Humbleness   Host: the firm at the third place

The firm at the third place is the only yang element of the gua. Obtaining the correct place but staying at the lower position, it is an image of humbleness.

Normally the third place is an unfavorable place. *The Great Treatise* says, "The third usually has misfortune . . ." But this one is among the most auspicious. Because of its humbleness, even though located in an unfavorable situation, it still brings good fortune.

16. ䷏ Delight   Host: the firm at the fourth place

Neither central nor correct, the yang situates at the fourth place, yet all yin correspond to it. This makes him delight. The Commentary on the Decision says, "The firm meets with corresponds. Its will is fulfilled. Acting in accord with time and moving forward. This is Delight."

17. ䷐ Following   Host: the firm in the initial place

The theme of the gua is the firm willing to place himself under the yielding and follow the yielding with delight. The Commentary on the Decision says, "The firm comes and places itself under the yielding. Moving with delight, it is Following. All under Heaven follow the course of time. Great indeed is the significance of time!"

18. ☶☴ Remedying   Host: The firm at the top place

The Commentary on the Decision says, "The firm is above and the yielding below. Gentle and standing still. This is Remedying. The Commentary says again, "Remedying. Sublimely prosperous and smooth. The firm on the top stands at the end of the gua, there will be a new beginning."

19. ☷☱ Approaching   Host: the firm at the initial place
                                                the firm at the second place

There are two yang elements at the bottom. The Commentary on the Decision says, "Approaching. The firm are advancing and growing."

20. ☴☷ Watching   Host: the firm at the fifth place
                                                the firm at the top place

There are two yang elements above. The Commentary on the Decision says, "The great virtue to be watched is above, gentle and obedient. In the central and correct place, he exhibits his virtue to all beings under Heaven."

21. ☲☳ Eradicating   Host: the firm at the fourth place

The structure of the gua looks like an open mouth with an obstruction. The Commentary on the Decision says, "There is something in the mouth. It is called Eradication. Through eradication, prosperity and smoothness come."

The firm at the fourth place is the obstruction in the mouth.

22. ☶☲ Adorning   Host: the yielding at the second place
                                                the firm at the top place

The yielding at the second place is the only yin element in the lower gua; the firm at the top place is the only yang element in the upper gua. They are the hosts of the gua. The Commentary on the Decision says, "The yielding descends to adorn the firm . . . The firm ascends to adorn the yielding." It is to explain that Adorning comes from Advance ☷☲ (11), that the yielding on the top of Advance comes down to the second place; and the firm at the second place goes up to the top; then Advance becomes Adorning.

23. ☶☷ Falling Away   Host: the firm at the top place

The firm on the top is the only yang element in the gua. The remaining five yin elements are moving forward, trying to overthrow the yang. The Commentary on the Decision says, "Falling Away is decaying. The yielding wants to change the firm . . . Little fellows are growing and extending. In a decaying situation, only the firm on the top place stands firm; it is the only fruit that remains uneaten."

24. ☷☳ Turning Back   Host: the firm at the initial place

The firm at the initial place is the only yang element in the gua. The Commentary on the Decision says, "Turning Back is prosperous and smooth. The firm returns . . . The firm is growing and extending. From this gua, one can see the heart of Heaven and Earth."

25. ☰☳ Without Falsehood   Host: the firm at the initial place
                                               the firm at the fifth place

Truth should start at the very beginning and carry on to the end. There are two hosts in this gua. The Commentary on the Decision says, "Without Falsehood. The firm comes from the outer and becomes the host of the inner. Movement with strength; the firm is at the central place and has a correspondent. Great prosperity and smoothness through its correctness, this is the will of Heaven." This indicates that Without Falsehood ☰☳ comes from Contention ☰☵ (6). That, the firm on the bottom of Without Falsehood ☰☳ came from the second line of Contention ☰☵. Then the lower gua of Without Falsehood becomes Thunder, which signifies taking action. Thus The Commentary says, "Movement with strength . . ."

26. ䷙ Great Accumulation   Host: the firm at the top place

The Commentary on the Decision says, "The firm on the top honors the virtuous. He is able to keep his strength still."

27. ䷚ Nourishing   Host: the firm at the top place

The firm at the top place is the source of nourishment. The Commentary on the Decision says, "Heaven and Earth nourish all beings. The holy sages nourish the virtuous, and thus reach all. Great indeed is nourishing in its time!" The firm on the top indicates a sage.

28. ䷛ Great Exceeding   Host: the firm at the second place
the firm at the fifth place

The Commentary on the Decision says, "The ridgepole sags; two ends are weak. The firm exceeds the yielding at the central place." There are two different opinions about the hosts. Some say the yielding at the initial and the yielding on the top are the hosts. Others prefer the firm at the second place and the firm at the fifth place to be the hosts. This piece regards the central places to be the host.

29. ䷜ Darkness   Host: the firm at the second place
the firm at the fifth place

The hosts of this gua lie in the two central places. The Commentary on the Decision says, "Darkness is doubled. Dangers succeed one after another . . . . Rely on your heart and mind. The firms are in the central places. Deeds will be honored. Going forward, there is success."

30. ䷝ Brightness   Host: the yielding at the second place
the yielding at the fifth place

The hosts of this gua lie in the two central places. The Commentary on the Decision says, "Doubled Brightness attaches to what is correct . . . The yielding attaches to the central and correct places."

THE LOWER CANON

31. ䷞ Mutual Influence   Host: the firm at the third place
                                           the yielding at the top place

There are three different opinions about the host of this gua. The first opinion prefers the firm at the fifth place and the yielding at the second place. Both of them are central and correct, and correspond to each other.

The second opinion prefers the firm at the fourth place, because it is in the middle of the gua, equivalent to the heart in a body. The heart is the source of mutual influence, and mutual influence should radiate from the heart.

The third opinion prefers the yielding at the top and the firm at the third place. Although they are not central, both of them are in the correct place and correspondent to each other. This, I believe, is the proper choice, because The Commentary on the Decision says, "The gentle is above, the firm below. The love of the two induces and corresponds; a union is formed."

32. ䷟ Long Lasting   Host: the firm at the second place

The firm at the second place is at the center of the lower gua. Only by walking in the central way can one last long. The yielding at the fifth place is weak (yin), thus the firm at the second place is better suited to be the host.

33. ䷠ Retreat   Host: the yielding at the second place

The Commentary on the Decision says, "The firm is at the right place and properly corresponds. It accords with time." It denotes that the yielding at the second place corresponds to the firm at the fifth place. Both of them are central and correct. Corresponding to each other, they bring about a favorable situation. Retreat is due to the two yin elements on the bottom, which proceed forward and force the yang elements to retreat. Of the two yin elements, the yielding at the second place is central and correct. It is more suitable to be the host.

34. ䷡ Great Strength   Host: the firm at the fourth place

There are four yang elements in the gua. The Commentary on the Decision says, "Great Strength. Favorable to be steadfast and upright; what is great should be righteous. When righteousness is great, the truth of Heaven and Earth can be seen." The firm at the fourth place is the head of the four yang elements. It deserves the dominant position.

35. ䷢ Proceeding Forward   Host: the yielding at the fifth place

The yielding at the fifth place is at the central place of the upper gua, Li ☲.

Li ☲ is the symbol of the sun. The image of the gua as a whole is that of a sun rising over the earth. The Commentary on the Decision says, "The bright is appearing over the earth. The submissive is clinging to the brilliant. The gentle is proceeding and moving upward."

36. ䷣ Brilliance Injured   Host: the yielding at the second place
                                             the yielding at the fifth place

The two central places of the gua, the second and the fifth places are occupied by yin elements. The gua represents a time of darkness and hardship as experienced by King Wen and Ji Tze, a sage of the Shang dynasty. Thus these two principal lines represent the two sages, who suffered in this dark age.

37. ䷤ Household   Host: the yielding at the second place
                                             the firm at the fifth place

The gua should have two hosts, because a man and a woman compose a household. The Commentary on the Decision says, "The woman obtains the proper place within; the man obtain a proper place without." Within is the inner gua; without is the outer gua. The firm at the fifth place is the husband; the yielding at the second place is the wife.

38. ䷥ Diversity   Host: the firm at the second place
                                             the yielding at the fifth place

The Commentary on the Decision says, "The yielding advances and moves upward. It attains the central place and corresponds to the firm." The

Commentary refers to the yielding at the fifth place, although incorrect but central, it corresponds to the firm at the second place.

39. ䷜ Hardship   Host: the firm at the fifth place

The Commentary on the Decision says, "Danger in front. Seeing the danger and knowing to stand still." The Commentary continues, "Going forward obtains the central place . . . Favorable to see a great person." The central place denotes the fifth place, and the great person denotes the yang element at the fifth place.

40. ䷧ Relief   Host: the firm at the second place
                                             the yielding at the fifth place

The gua represents a humble leader working with an able subordinate, to overcome hardship together. The yielding at the fifth place is the humble King, and the firm at the second place is the able official. The Commentary on the Decision says, "Danger produces motion. Through motion, danger is removed. Going forward, win the multitude. Returning back brings good fortune. He obtains the central position."

41. ䷨ Decreasing   Host: the yielding at the fifth place

The Commentary on the Decision says, "To decrease what is lower is to increase what is above. The way is to benefit the above." In this case, "below" refers to ordinary people and "above" refers to the king. The yielding at the fifth place is above, at the king's place. It is the host of the gua.

42. ䷩ Increasing   Host: the firm at the initial place

The Commentary on the Decision says, "To decrease what is above is to increase what is below. The joy of the people is boundless. Increase of what is below comes from what is above. Its way is greatly brightened." What is below is the firm at the initial place, indicating the ordinary people.

43. ䷪ Eliminating   Host: the yielding at the top place

The Commentary on the Decision says, "It is a resolution to eliminate something. The firms eliminate the yielding." The five yang elements eliminate the only yin element, which is at the top and is the host.

44. ☴ Encountering   Host: the yielding at the initial place

The Commentary on the Decision says. "Encountering. Meet someone unexpectedly. The yielding encounters the firms." The sole yin element approaches five yang elements. It is the host of the gua.

45. ☱ Bringing Together   Host: the yielding at the second place
                                       the firm at the fifth place

The Commentary on the Decision says, "The firm is central and has correspondence. Therefore people come and assemble together." There are two yang elements that reside in high positions. One is the king, and the other is the minister. They are both working hard to bring people together.

46. ☷ Growing Upward   Host: the yielding at the initial place

The Commentary on the Decision says, "The yielding ascends in accord with time." It indicates the yielding at the initial place, which is the root of growth. Since growth starts from the bottom, this line is the host.

47. ☱ Exhausting   Host: the firm at the fifth place

In an exhausting situation one should still seek what is prosperous and smooth. The Commentary on the Decision says, "Facing danger, still be joyous. In an exhausting situation one does not lose his prosperity and smoothness. Only the superior person is able to do it." Obviously this refers to the firm at the fifth place.

48. ☵ Replenishing   Host: the firm at the fifth place

The name of the gua refers to a well. In ancient times a well was a place for people to replenlish themselves after a day's hard work. A well provides water. The firm at the fifth place lies in the central place of the upper gua, Water. The ideal society as pictured by the ancient sages was one in which the king nourishs and replenishes his subordinates, and the subordinates respect the king.

49. ䷰ Abolishing the Old   Host: the firm at the fifth place

The Commentary on the Decision says, "Tang and Wu abolished the old and brought about the new. They obeyed the will of Heaven in accord with the wishes of people." Tang and Wu are the two greatest kings in Chinese history. Only a great person, firm and strong, central and correct, and in a supreme position is capable of being the leader during a time of great change.

50. ䷱ Establishing the New   Host: the yielding at the fifth place

The name of the gua is Ding, a cauldron. In ancient times, when a new dynasty began or a new emperor was enthroned, the first thing to do was to cast a new cauldron and inscribe the new constitution on it, symbolizing the beginning of a new era. The emperor employed the cauldron to prepare sacrificial offerings to the lord of Heaven and to nourish the wise and virtuous. The Commentary on the Decision says, "The yielding advances and goes upward. It obtains the central position." The yielding at the fifth place represents the person who takes charge of the ceremony.

51. ䷲ Taking Action   Host: the firm at the initial place

Taking Action has two yang elements, both of which could be the host. However, the action starts at the bottom and moves upward. Thus, the firm at the initial place is more suitable to be the host.

52. ䷳ Keeping Still   Host: the firm on the top place

Keeping Still has two yang elements, both of which could be the host. However, the firm at the third place is still in motion, while the yang energy at the top is at rest. Thus, this line is the host.

53. ䷴ Developing Gradually   Host: the yielding at the second place
                                          the firm at the fifth place

Developing Gradually employs an analogy of a marrying maiden to describe a gradual process of development. The yielding at the second place represents a marrying maiden; the firm at the fifth place represents the prospective husband. They are the hosts of the gua.

54. ䷵ Marrying Maiden　　　　Host: the yielding at the third place
　　　　　　　　　　　　　　　　the yielding at the fifth place

The Commentary on the Decision says, "Marrying off a young maiden. Moving forward: misfortune; places are not correct. Nothing is favorable; yielding are mounting on the firms." The yin element at the third and the fifth places are both yielding, and both are mounted on the firm. Thus, both of them are the hosts.

55. ䷶ Abundance　　　　　　Host: the yielding at the fifth place

The Commentary on the Decision says, "The king reaches this point. He values abundance and greatness. Do not worry. Be like the sun at noon. One should radiate his light on earth." The yielding at the fifth place is central and in the supreme place. Here it can be as brilliant as the sun.

56. ䷷ Traveling　　　　　　Host: the yielding at the fifth place

The Commentary on the Decision says, "The yielding is central in the outer; it follows the solids. Keeping the still and clinging to the brilliance, there is chance for a little prosperity and smoothness." The yielding at the fifth place is in the outer gua, and also in the middle of Li, Brilliance. Obviously it is the host.

57. ䷸ Proceeding Humbly　　Host: the firm at the fifth place

There are two yielding lines, one at the bottom of the lower gua, the other at the bottom of the upper gua, both could be the host. However, The Commentary on the Decision says, "The firm proceeds humbly to the central and to the correct position. Its goal is to be filfilled." This refers to the firm at the fifth place.

58. ䷹ Joyful   Host: the firm at the second place
                                                the firm at the fifth place

The Commentary on the Decision says, "The solid are in the center, and the yielding at the outer places. Joy is favorable to being steadfast and upright. It is acting in accordance to the will of Heaven and in correspondence with the wish of people." The firm at the second place is central. The firm at the fifth place is central and correct. They are both the hosts of the gua.

59. ䷺ Dispersing   Host: the yielding at the fourth place
                                                the firm at the fifth place.

The Commentary on the Decision says, "The firm comes without hindrance. The yielding is at the proper place. It goes out to meet his similarity above. The king arrives at the temple. He is in the central place." The firm at the fifth place is the king who approaches the temple to connect himself with the lord of Heaven. During the time of Dispersing, he is the only one who, being in the honored place, is able to establish order. The yielding at the fourth place is the minister. He is at his proper place. Both of them are appropriate hosts.

60. ䷻ Restricting   Host: the firm at the fifth place

The Commentary on the Decision says, "Passing danger with joy, carry out restriction in the proper position. From the correct and central place, his advance is without limitation." Only the firm at the fifth place is central and correct. Only a person of supreme wisdom and in an honorable place is able to adjust right and wrong and practice the Tao of restriction. Obviously the firm at the fifth place is the host.

61. ䷼ Innermost Sincerity   Host: the firm at the second place
                                                the firm at the fifth place

The Commentary on the Decision says, "Innermost Sincerity. The yielding are within, and the solids obtain the central places." This leads to two different opinions. One holds that the innermost sincerity should radiate from the heart. According to this idea, the host of the gua should be the two yin elements in the middle of the gua. However, sincerity should be solid in the heart. According to this idea, two yang elements in the central places should be the hosts. The Commentary on the Decision says, "Innermost Sincerity and trustworthiness are favorable with steadfastness and uprightness. It responds to the principle of Heaven." Therefore, this book prefers the firm at the second place and the firm at the fifth place as the hosts.

62.☲ Little Exceeding   Host: the yielding at the second place
                                          the yielding at the fifth place

According to King Wen's Decision, this gua gives warning against overdoing. The Commentary on the Decision says, "The yielding attain the central places. There is good fortune in dealing with small affairs. The solids are neither central nor correct. Great affairs should not be dealt with." The yielding at the second place and the yielding at the fifth place are in the central position. They are the hosts.

63. ☷ Already Fulfilled   Host: the yielding at the second place

The Commentary on the Decision says, "Beginning: good fortune, for the yielding is in the central." There are three yielding lines in this gua, but only the yielding line at the second place is central. It is the host.

64. ☶ Not Yet Fulfilled   Host: the yielding at the fifth place

The Commentary on the Decision says, "Not Yet Fulfilled. There is prosperity and smoothness for the yielding to attain the central place." There are three yielding lines in this gua, but only the yielding line at the fifth place is central. It is the host.

* * *

For the convenience of the reader, all sixty-four gua are summarized below, in groupings of ratio of yin to yang.

Two gua – the ratio of yin and yang element in each gua is 1:0

☰ Initiating (1)   ☷ Responding (2)

Twelve gua – the ratio of yin and yang element in each gua is 1:5

☷ Multitude (7)   ☵ Union (8)
☴ Little Accumulation (9)   ☱ Fulfillment (10)
☰ Seeking Harmony (13)   ☲ Great Harvest (14)
☶ Humbleness (15)   ☳ Delight (16)
☶ Falling Away (23)   ☳ Turning Back (24)
☱ Eliminating (43)   ☴ Encountering (44)

Thirty gua – the ratio of yin and yang element in each gua is 2:4

☵ Beginning (3)   ☶ Childhood (4)
☵ Needing (5)   ☵ Contention (6)
☱ Approaching (19)   ☴ Watching (20)
☳ Without Falsehood (25)   ☶ Great Accumulation (26)
☳ Nourishing (27)   ☱ Great Exceeding (28)
☵ Darkness (29)   ☲ Brightness (30)
☶ Retreat (33)   ☳ Great Strength (34)
☶ Proceeding Forward (35)   ☲ Brilliance Injured (36)
☴ Household (37)   ☱ Diversity (38)
☵ Hardship (39)   ☳ Relief (40)
☱ Bringing Together (45)   ☷ Growing Upward (46)
☱ Abolishing the Old (49)   ☲ Establishing the New (50)
☳ Taking Action (51)   ☶ Keeping Still (52)
☴ Proceeding Humbly (57)   ☱ Joyful (58)
☴ Innermost Sincerity (61)   ☳ Little Exceeding (62)

Twenty gua – the ratio of yin and yang element in each gua is 3:3

䷜ Advance (11)   ䷋ Hindrance (12)
䷐ Following (17)   ䷑ Remedying (18)
䷓ Eradicating (21)   ䷕ Adorning (22)
䷞ Mutual Influence (31)   ䷟ Long Lasting (32)
䷨ Decreasing (41)   ䷩ Increasing (42)
䷮ Exhausting (47)   ䷯ Replenishing (48)
䷴ Developing Gradually (53) ䷵ Marrying Maiden (54)
䷶ Abundance (55)   ䷷ Traveling (56)
䷺ Dispersing (59)   ䷻ Restricting (60)
䷾ Already Fulfilled (63)   ䷿ Not Yet Fulfilled (64)

5

周 易 的 卦 序
The Sequence of the I Ching

Although King Wen's sequence of the sixty-four gua is thoughtfully arranged, unfortunately, most Western I Ching scholars believe that the textual sequence of King Wen's arrangement of the sixty-four gua is random. The consensus is that no rationale exists for arranging the gua in such an order.

For instance, Richard Wilhelm says,

> The Ninth Wing, Hsu Gua Chuan 序卦传, the Sequence or Order of the Hexagrams, offers a rather unconvincing explanation of the present sequence of the hexagrams. It is interesting only because the names of the hexagrams are sometimes given peculiar interpretations that are undoubtedly based on ancient tradition. (*The I Ching or Book of Changes, p. 260*)

Derek Walters says,

> The order of the hexagrams is . . . an apparently random one (at least no one has yet convincingly explained the reason for the sequence). (*The Tai Hsuan Ching: The Hidden Classic, p. 8*)

James Legge says,

> The sixth Appendix is the Treatise on the Sequence of the
> Hexagrams . . . The author of this treatise endeavors to
> explain the meaning of the names, and also the sequence of
> the figures, or how it is that the idea of the one leads on to
> that of the next . . . The connection between any two is
> generally sufficiently close; but on the whole the essays . . .
> resemble 'a heap of oriental pearls at random strung.' (*I Ching,*
> *Book of Changes, p. 54*)

I think that besides King Wen's personal philosophy, he strictly followed
Fu Xi's circular arrangement of the eight primary gua. Unfortunately, most
Western I Ching scholars have had no opportunity to study the numerology
of the I Ching. As a result, there should be no blame placed on them for their
ignorance regarding the underlying reasoning for the sequence of the gua.

King Wen's Philosophy

When King Wen rearranged the sequence of the I Ching to the present order,
it was based upon his life philosophy – personal and political.

King Wen deeply believed in the philosophy of *the unity between Heaven*
and Humanity, in which the purpose of Heaven and the purpose of human
beings should be harmoniously united. In other words, the goal of a human
being is to follow the will of Heaven and the wishes of humankind. This philosophy was formed through profound study of Fu Xi's eight primary gua, plus
the other two pre-existing *I* – the *Lian Shang I* 连山易 and the *Gui Zang I* 归藏
易. In addition, his arrangement of the gua reflected his deep contemplation of
history and his own life experience during seven years of confinement by the
last emperor of the Shang dynasty, the tyrant of Shang.

King Wen did not overtly express his philosophy in the text, but it
permeates the whole book, especially as revealed in its structure. He divided the book into two parts, the Upper Canon and the Lower Canon.
The Upper Canon emphasizes shedding light upon Heaven, the yang aspect of natural phenomena, the Tao of Heaven. The Lower Canon stresses

shedding light upon Humanity, the yin aspect of natural phenomena, the Tao of Humanity.

King Wen arranged Qian ☰ *Initiating* as the first gua and Kun ☷ *Responding* as the second gua. Qian *is* the initiator, representing the function of Heaven, while Kun is the responder, representing the function of Earth and Humanity. The Decision he wrote for the second gua, Responding, states that the female horse should be submissive to the male horse's initiative; this is to say that yin should follow yang. This is the law of nature, the law of Heaven and Earth, and the law of Humanity.

Eight Primary Gua

Referring back to what we elaborated in Chapter 3, recall that the I Ching is a book of symbols. In fact, long before it became a book of written language, I Ching existed in the form of symbols only. Symbols are still the **key** to a true understanding of the I Ching. The symbols are in the form of gua. Most English texts translate gua as "trigram" or "hexagram" depending on the context. In Chinese, gua means "hanging up." That is, hanging up the symbols for people to see, so that they know how to act to receive good fortune or to avoid misfortune.

The Great Treatise on the I Ching, written by Confucius, says:

> *In I there is Tai Chi.*
> *Tai Chi generates two primary energies.*
> *Two Primary energies generate four primary symbols.*
> *Four primary symbols generate eight primary gua.*

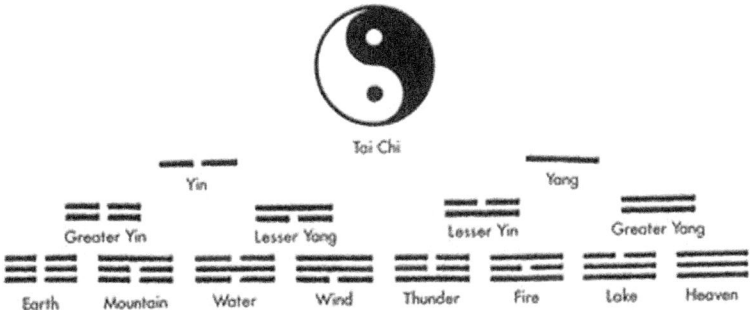

The Great Treatise states these principles, but gives no further illustration. Not until fifteen hundred years after Confucius, in the Song dynasty (960 – 1279 A. D.), did scholars of the Symbol and Number School at last create a graphic illustration of what *The Great Treatise* states.

Fu Xi's Eight Primary Gua

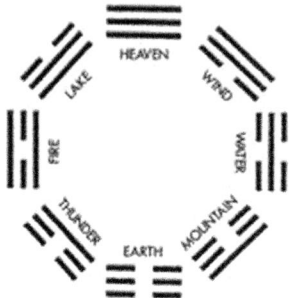

It is believed that Fu Xi created this circular arrangement of the eight primary gua. He sensed that heaven was always there above him, so he put the symbol of Heaven ☰ at the top. (On ancient Chinese maps, south always appears on the top.) Because he knew earth was always beneath him, he put the symbol of Earth ☷ at the bottom.

Between Heaven and Earth there were two obvious objects, the sun and the moon. Therefore he hung the symbol of the Sun ☲ in the east and the symbol of Moon ☵ in the west. As the sun is a source of heat and light, he decided that its symbol also represented Fire. The moon, however, does not radiate heat and light, so he associated it with the symbol of Water, as water is cold and its character is opposite to that of fire.

There were two more items that drew Fu Xi's attention, the thunderstorm and the wind, which, he realized, had tremendous energy. When the wind was not harsh and the thunderstorm was timely, they were favorable to the crops; they always worked together in close relationship in everyday lives. Therefore Fu Xi hung the symbol of Thunder ☳ in the northeast and the symbol of Wind ☴ in the southwest.

Finally, he completed the sequence by arranging the symbol of Mountain ☶ in the northwest and the symbol of Lake ☱ in the southeast, as the Chinese associated activating energy with mountains and soothing energy with lakes.

Fu Xi's eight primary gua contained the eight directions. Heaven ☰ and Earth ☷, Fire ☲ and Water ☵ represent the four directions, south, north, east and west. These directions serve as the major framework of the whole book.

Following the cardinal directions, King Wen placed Heaven ☰ and Earth ☷ at the beginning of the book, and named them Qian and Kun, which mean Initiating and Responding. These two gua act as the introduction to I Ching.

He placed Darkness ䷜ and Brightness ䷝ at the end of *the Upper Canon*, and named them Kan and Li, which symbolize the moon and the sun, or Darkness and Brightness.

Already Fulfilled ䷾ and Not Yet Fulfilled ䷿, the two most balanced and harmonious combinations of the yin and yang, were placed at the end of the book, where they serve as the conclusion. Both of them are also made up of Water and Fire.

Fu Xi's four diagonal directions are represented by Mountain ☶ and Lake ☱, Thunder ☳ and Wind ☴. Mountain represents northwest, Lake represents southeast, Thunder represents northeast, and Wind represents southwest.

In *the Lower Canon*, King Wen placed the combination of Lake ☱ and Mountain ☶ as the first gua and called it Xian ䷞, which means "Mutual Influence." He placed the combination of Thunder ☳ and Wind ☴ as the second gua of *the Lower Canon* and named it Heng ䷟, which means "Long Lasting."

In this way King Wen strictly followed Fu Xi's guidance and created an arrangement in which there are profound hidden meanings.

Qian ☰ is yang, representing the initiative power of Heaven; while Kun ☷ is yin, representing the responsive power of Earth. When Qian ☰ and Kun ☷, Heaven and Earth, harmoniously function together, the myriad beings are created and life is sustained. Therefore, King Wen placed Qian ☰, which operates as the guiding principle of the thirty gua of *the Upper Canon*, as the start of the sixty-four gua, followed by Kun ☷, which serves as the guiding principle of the thirty-four gua of *the Lower Canon.*

Moreover, the significance of the first gua, Qian ☰, is to explore natural phenomenon, the Tao of Heaven. The significance of the second gua, Kun ☷, is to explore social phenomenon, the Tao of Humanity. The Tao of Heaven is initiation; the Tao of Humanity is response and submission. As a human being, one should be submissive to Heaven's function and be responsive to Heaven's initiation. A Chinese proverb says,

> Heaven is vast and Earth is lasting.
> When sun and moon come together,
> Brightness becomes brilliant.

Therefore, this truth is as "vast" as Heaven and as "lasting" as Earth, and also as "bright and brilliant" as the sun and the moon.

The union of Heaven ☰ and Earth ☷, or the union of Initiating ☰ and Responding ☷, is the model for the union of male and female. The ancient Chinese considered no other relationship in human society to be more significant than that between husband and wife. The relationship should be mutually influencing and long lasting. Thus, *the Lower Canon* begins with Xian ䷞ and Heng ䷟ – Mutual Influence and Long Lasting, which represent the harmonious, supportive and loving relationship of a man and a woman.

The book ends with Ji Ji ䷾ and Wei Ji ䷿, both of which are the combination of Water ☵ and Fire ☲. Ji Ji ䷾, Already Fulfilled is Water ☵ above, Fire ☲ below; while Wei Ji ䷿, Not Yet Fulfilled is Fire ☲ above and Water ☵ below. In ancient China, Fire ☲ represented the sun and Water ☵ represented the moon. These two characters together mean brightness. Ji Ji ䷾ and Wei Ji ䷿ represent the endless cycle of natural phenomena and human affairs from already-fulfilled to not-yet-fulfilled, and back to already-fulfilled.

King Wen's arrangement of the sixty-four gua is such that the odd-numbered gua and the even-numbered gua immediately adjacent to it form a pair. The even-numbered gua is either an *inverse* (upside-down) form or an *opposite* (yin and yang reversed) from the odd-numbered gua preceding it. In this way, the sixty-four gua are closely linked in a continuous wavelike sequence. Based upon this principle, the sixty-four gua are arranged as follows in the list below: the pairs of gua with inverse form are in plain text font; those with opposite form are indicated by italic type.

The Upper Canon

Odd-Numbered Gua   Even-Numbered Gua

Odd-Numbered Gua	Even-Numbered Gua
1. *Initiating*	2. *Responding*
3. Beginning	4. Childhood
5. Needing	6. Contention
7. Multitude	8. Union
9. Little Accumulation	10. Fulfillment
11. Advance	12. Hindrance
13. Seeking Harmony	14. Great Harvest
15. Humbleness	16. Delight
17. Following	18. Remedying
19. Approaching	20. Watching
21. Eradicating	22. Adorning
23. Falling Away	24. Turning Back
25. Without Falsehood	26. Great Accumulation
27. *Nourishing*	28. *Great Exceeding*
29. *Darkness*	30. *Brightness*

The Lower Canon

Odd-Numbered Gua   Even-Numbered Gua

Odd-Numbered Gua	Even-Numbered Gua
31. Mutual Influence	32. Long Lasting
33. Retreat	34. Great Strength
35. Proceeding Forward	36. Brilliance Injured
37. Household	38. Diversity

39. Hardship	䷦	䷧	40. Relief
41. Decreasing	䷨	䷩	42. Increasing
43. Eliminating	䷪	䷫	44. Encountering
45. Bringing Together	䷬	䷭	46. Growing Forward
47. Exhausting	䷮	䷯	48. Replenishing
49. Abolishing the Old	䷰	䷱	50. Establishing the New
51. Taking Action	䷲	䷳	52. Keeping Still
53. Developing Gradually	䷴	䷵	54. Marrying Maiden
55. Abundance	䷶	䷷	56. Traveling
57. Proceeding Humbly	䷸	䷹	58. Joyful
59. Dispersing	䷺	䷻	60. Restricting
61. *Innermost Sincerity*	䷼	䷽	62. *Little Exceeding*
63. Already Fulfilled	䷾	䷿	64. Not Yet Fulfilled

Hidden Balance of the Gua

The I Ching presents the phenomena of the interchange, interaction, growth and decline of yin and yang. There is always a tendency toward balance in the interaction and interchange of the two. When either yin or yang reaches the extreme, it is out of balance and a dramatic change takes place by the alternating of the original force to its opposite. The fluctuation seeks balance. When yin and yang meet, there is balance. It is the law of nature that the evolution and development of Heaven and Earth, and all the beings in between, occurs through the process of attaining balance.

King Wen's arrangement of the sixty-four gua embeds a hidden balance of the numbers of the yao or lines. There are thirty gua in the Upper Canon and thirty-four gua in the Lower Canon. It seems out of balance. However, this imbalance is only in appearance. Deep in its structure as a whole, there is balance.

Among the sixty-four gua there are fifty-six that can be turned upside down to form new gua. These are called inverse gua. For instance, when the third gua, Beginning ䷂, is turned upside down, it becomes the fourth gua, Childhood ䷃. The appearances of these two gua seem different, but the structure of each – the number of their yin and yang lines – remains the same.

In the Upper Canon there are six gua that, when turned upside down, remain the same:

Qian	(1)	䷀	Initiating
Kun	(2)	䷁	Responding
Yi	(27)	䷚	Nourishing
Da Guo	(28)	䷛	Great Exceeding
Kan	(29)	䷜	Darkness
Li	(30)	䷝	Brightness

As a result, the thirty gua in the Upper Canon, minus these six, result in twenty-four gua that have inverse forms. Because these gua have reciprocal structures and equal numbers of yin and yang lines, the twenty-four invertible gua produce only twelve distinct patterns of gua (24 divided by 2 equals 12). Considering the additional six non-invertible gua, there are a total of eighteen distinct structures of gua in the Upper Canon (12 plus 6 equals 18).

In the Lower Canon, there are two gua that, when turned upside down, remain the same:

Zhong Fu	(61)	䷼	Innermost Sincerity
Xiao Guo	(62)	䷽	Little Exceeding

Consequently, thirty-four gua minus these two gua without inverse forms result in thirty-two gua (34 minus 2 equals 32) that have inverse forms. The 32 invertible gua produce sixteen distinct patterns of gua (32 divided by 2 equals 16). Therefore, two gua with no inverse forms plus sixteen gua with inverse forms make eighteen (16 plus 2 equals 18) distinct structures of gua in the Lower Canon. Thus, both the Upper Canon and the Lower Canon contain eighteen distinct structures of gua.

Hidden Balance of the Yao

There is also a hidden balance in the number of yao, or lines, in King Wen's arrangement.

- There are 30 gua in the Upper Canon containing a total of 94 yin lines and 86 yang lines.
- Calculating 94 yin lines minus 86 yang lines, demonstrates there are 8 more yin lines than yang lines.
- There are 34 gua in the Lower Canon containing a total of 106 yang lines and 98 yin lines.
- Calculating 106 yang lines minus 98 yin lines, reveals there are 8 more yang lines than yin lines.

Over all, there is still a balanced number of yin and yang lines in the entire book.

Considering only the 18 distinct patterns of gua in the Upper and Lower Canon.

- There are 56 yin lines and 52 yang lines in the Upper Canon.
- Calculating 56 yin lines minus 52 yang lines, shows there are 4 more yin lines more than yang lines.
- There are 56 yang lines and 52 yin lines in the Lower Canon.
- Calculating 56 yang lines minus 52 yin lines, demonstrates there are 4 more yang lines more than yin lines.

Again, the structure of the book exhibits a balanced number of lines.

An Unchangeable Truth

Westerners translated the title of I Ching as *The Book of Changes* and nick-named it, *A Book of Wisdom*. But, according to my personal view, they did not know what "changes" the book would produce, and what "wisdom" the book would suggest.

To the Chinese, the *I of the Zhou Dynasty* 周易 has three qualities: the first is changing 变易, the second is "easy to change 简易", and the third is "un-changeable 不易."

In other words, what the I Ching teaches is how to conduct oneself to deal with people or things appropriately according to the time and the situation. What the I Ching teaches is simple to understand and easy to follow, and it is unchangeable truth.

One of the unchangeable truths is concealed deeply in the sequence. A time-situation represented by one of the two gua Initiating ☰ or Responding ☷ can proceed through a series of sixty-three changes, in the case of Initiating, or sixty-two changes in the case of Responding, to either Already Fulfilled ䷾ or Not Yet Fulfilled ䷿ respectively. In this manner, the most unharmonized, unbalanced and non-corresponding gua, Qian ☰ or Kun ☷, becomes one of the most harmonized, balanced, and corresponding gua, Already Fulfilled ䷾ or Not Yet Fulfilled ䷿.

The Chinese think that this is the most harmonious situation and crown it "Super Harmony 太和."

So, it can be seen that the comments of many Western scholars, to the effect that there is no reasoning underlying the sequence of the gua as established by King Wen, are quite unjustified. Beginning with the profound selection of the pair of gua Initiating and Responding as the introduction to the text, the sequence of the gua, upon careful study, reveals great philosophical depth. Intensive study of the sequence of the gua also illuminates numerological relationships, which inform the ideal, harmonious relationships of Heaven, Earth and Humanity.

6

易经的入门
The Gateway of the I Ching

The first and the second hexagrams of the I Ching are the gateway to understanding the I Ching. The Great Commentary of the I Ching says,

> Qian 乾 and Qun 坤, are they really the gateway of the I?
> Qian 乾 and Kun 坤, do they really enclose the treasures of the I?

Wang Fu Ze 王夫子 (1619 – 1692), a great scholar between the Ming and Qing dynasties, asserted the key to explaining the essence of the I Ching of the Zhou dynasty by putting Qian and Kun side by side. He understood precisely that the principles of Qian and Kun together represent the principle of *I*, or the *Tao of I*.

In 1989, at the age of eighty-seven, Master Jin Jing-fang 金景芳 (1902 – 2001), with his student Lu Shao-gang 吕绍纲, wrote *The Comprehensive Interpretation on the I Ching of the Zhou Dynasty* 周易全解. He wrote approximately 30,000 Chinese characters to explain Qian 乾, nearly 20,000 characters to explain Kun 坤 and only about 5,000 characters for each of the rest of the hexagrams. In the system of the I Ching, only Qian and Kun have an extra seventh line, and only Qian and Kun have an extra Wen Yan 文言 – the seventh wing of the Ten Wings – to provide details to elucidate the two hexagrams. This underlines the importance of Qian and Kun for understanding the I Ching.

The Central Theme of the I Ching

"Zhou I" is the simplified term for the I Ching of the Zhou Dynasty 周易. Its purpose is to expound the Tao of I 易道. The Tao of I includes the Tao of Heaven 天道, the Tao of Earth 地道, and the Tao of Humanity 人道.

Then, how does I Ching express the Tao of I? By means of symbols made up of a combination of six lines, each of either yin or yang character, together with the scripts explaining what they represent. The symbols are called "hexagrams." In Chinese, they are referred to as gua 卦.

The Great Commentary of the I Ching 周易大传 states, "One yin and one yang, this is what is called the Tao." The Tao is reflected in the changes of the yin and the yang elements. What the I Ching discusses is the nature of the changes of the yin and the yang elements; the law of the changes of the yin and the yang elements forms the Tao of I. The Tao of I becomes the philosophy of the changes of the yin and the yang. Thus, many people call I Ching "The Book of Changes."

The Tao of I Is Profound

I Ching, The Book of Changes, is the oldest of the Chinese classics. Throughout its history, it has commanded unsurpassed prestige and popularity.

The most ancient Chinese library catalogue, known as *The Descriptive Accounts of Books in the Han Dynasty* 汉书艺文志, states, "The Tao of I is so profound that its authors included three saints and its generations of authors included three dynasties of remote antiquity."

Traditionally, I Ching was attributed to three authors in three remote antiquities. The first was Fu Xi 伏羲, a prehistoric chieftain in the age of ancient antiquity about 3,000 B.C. The second was King Wen 文王 and his son, Duke of Zhou 周公, in the age of middle antiquity about eleventh century B.C. The third was Confucius 孔子, a humanistic philosopher in the age of recent antiquity, about sixth and fifth century B.C. All of these names represent the most outstanding figures in the birth and development of Chinese culture.

The Source of Chinese Culture

Nowadays, China has more influence than ever upon the world, and more people all over the world are interested in China. In order to better understand China, it is necessary to better understand the source of Chinese culture.

It is believed that when Fu Xi drew the eight trigrams of the I Ching, he established the embryonic form of the Chinese written characters. When King Wen developed the Zhou I, this marked the beginning of Chinese culture. However, I Ching is not only the oldest Chinese classic; it has been held in highest esteem and even revered as the zenith of all classics since ancient times.

To the Chinese, "classic" refers to the Tao, the Truth. It is the Truth of the relationship between Heaven and Earth, including the Truth of Humanity. These books, which explain the Tao of Heaven, the Tao of Earth, and the Tao of Humanity, are called "classic." Classic refers to the most sacred wisdom and records, and the most authoritative source of all truth. To the Chinese, heavenly principles are also humanistic principles. The great idea of the unity of Heaven and Humanity 天人合一 permeates the I Ching from the beginning, all the way to its end.

Thousands of years ago, the authors of I Ching watched the heavenly phenomenon above and examined the earthly features below, and tried to thoroughly understand the conditions of myriad beings. They carefully studied periods of good fortune and bad fortune. They acknowledged what should change, how to change and what should not change. They had a good command of changes and expounded the models of understanding the changes, appropriately responding to the changes, and conforming to the norm of changing.

This philosophy of the unity of Heaven and Humanity is the foundation of Chinese traditional culture; it is the root of all spheres of Chinese learning, and thus the distinguishing feature of Chinese culture.

Tao of Heaven

The Commentary of the Symbol of the first hexagram Qian says,

> *Heaven acts with vitality and persistence.*
> *In correspondence with this,*
> *The superior person keeps himself vital without ceasing.*

When the ancients observed the alternating changes of day and night, the wane and wax of the moon, and the changes of the seasons, they perceived the vital and persistent motion of Heaven. They instructed people to follow the way of Heaven, keeping themselves vital without halting.

No Words Not Originating from Symbols

According to the great Master Shang Bing-he 尚秉和 (1870 – 1950), "I Ching is a book, first and foremost of symbols. All the associated words are derived from the symbols. There are no words associated with I Ching that do not originate from the symbols."

Within the six lines of a hexagram, the bottom two lines represent Earth. The top two lines represent Heaven. The middle two lines represent human beings.

The first hexagram uses six dragons as symbols to show the changing process or the *timing* of an event in differing situations.

About the first line, the Wen Yan (Confucius's Commentary on the Words of the Text) says,

> *Dragon lying low; do not use.*
> *Position is low.*

As the bottom two lines symbolize the Earth, then the bottom line represents the place underneath the Earth. Thus the book advises, "Do not use," because "the place is low."

The second line says,

> *Dragon arising in the field,*
> *A time for action is arriving.*

According to the symbol, the second line is at the surface of the Earth, thus the text says that the dragon has arisen in the field. In addition, the line lies in the middle of the lower trigram. The I Ching esteems the one who is walking in the central path. Therefore, the line advises that it is time to take action.

The third line says,

> *The superior person, all day long initiating, initiating,*
> *Proceeding according to the plan.*

Please notice that the text here mentions "the superior person"; this is because the third line and the fourth line are positions representing the human being. The third line is boding of misfortune, because it is situated on the top of the lower trigram, a position that had already passed the central place. Also, it is going to step into the bottom of the upper trigram, which is entirely a new situation, so the one at the third place should be very cautious.

The fourth line says,

> *Dragon chooses either leaping out of or resting in the abyss.*
> *It is making a trial of his strength.*

This line has reached the bottom of the upper trigram; the one at this line still belongs to the Human place. Usually the one at the fourth line has much to fear. For instance, the one here is not familiar with the new situation, and also the place is too close to the one at the fifth place. In the system of the I Ching, the fifth place is the supreme place for the king. Especially with a solid line at the fifth place, called "the supreme place of the Nine Fifth 九五之尊," this place represents the king. Thus, the one at the fourth place is making a trial of his strength – whether to leap or to stay. It is demonstrating that he is cautious.

The fifth line says,

> *Dragon flying in the sky.*
> *The superior position leading and administrating.*

The fifth line and the sixth line belong to the place of Heaven, so the text says that the dragon is flying in the sky. The fifth line is a yang element at a yang place; the place is correct, and also central. Thus, the one at this place is leading and administrating the whole surrounding. This is the most auspicious line of the hexagram – the place is right, the timing is right, and the situation is right.

The sixth line says,

> *Dragon becomes haughty. There is regret.*
> *Extremity brings calamity.*

This line ends the hexagram. According to the I Ching, when things have reached the extremity, changes are near at hand. So the text gives warning that extremity brings calamity.

From this hexagram, I Ching is sending a very important message: when one has reached a situation of being prosperous and successful, one should remain humble. "Humble" is the most auspicious hexagram with all lines auspicious, which means that humbleness is favorable in any situation.

There is a seventh line in both the first hexagram and the second hexagram, which is called "the use of the Nine" or "the use of the Six."

The seventh line says,

> *When all firms change to yielding,*
> *Great order is achieved across the land.*

In order to understand this explanation, we should refer to the original text, which says, "There appears a group of dragons without a chief. Good fortune."

The eighth wing, The Discussion of the Trigrams, says, "Qian is chief." "Without a chief" indicates that, when all the solid lines change to yielding lines, Qian becomes Kun. After Qian becomes Kun, there is no more Qian, which indicates that there is no more chief. So the text of the line says, "There appears a group of dragons without a chief." The extreme firmness has coupled with softness; now great order can be achieved across the land.

The Essence of the Second Hexagram

To understand the essence of the second hexagram of the Zhou I, we have to comprehend the background of the time in which it was composed – a period of great change in the history of China.

The sequence of the first hexagram, Qian, says, "After heaven and earth have come into existence, myriad beings are produced. Qian and Kun are the origin, the source of Creation." This exemplifies the cosmology of the people at that time.

According to *The Book of Rites of the Zhou Dynasty* 周礼, there were three I – the Lian Shan I, the Gui Zang I, and the Zhou I. The Lian Shang I was the I Ching of the Xia dynasty 夏代 (2100 B.C. – 1600 B.C.), which began with the hexagram Mountain – Mountain above, Mountain below, symbolizing "clouds come out of the mountains, and go on and on." We do not know what the author's intention was to make this arrangement.

The Gui Zang I was the I Ching of the Shang dynasty 商代 (1600 – 1100 B.C.). It began with the hexagram Earth – Earth above and Earth below. It symbolizes that all beings grow on earth, and finally will go back underneath the earth.

However, these two I Ching reflected that the people of both the Xia dynasty and the Shang dynasty did not understand the cosmology of myriad beings originating after Heaven and Earth had come into existence. Although the I Ching of the Shang dynasty arranged Kun and Qian as the first and second hexagrams, they did not have the concept that myriad beings were produced after Heaven and Earth had appeared.

A thousand years later, when the I Ching of the Zhou dynasty was composed, Qian, Initiating and Kun, Responding, were arranged to be the first and the second gua. It clearly put forward their cosmic view that it was Heaven and Earth that created the myriad beings.

In correspondence to *The Records of Historian* 史记, written by Sima Qian 司马迁 of the Han dynasty 汉代 (206 B.C. – 280 A.D.), in the section of *Hereditary of House of the Filial King of Liang*, it says, "The Queen mother told the King that she had heard that that the way of the Yin dynasty followed the system of maternal affinity 殷道亲亲 and that the way of the Zhou dynasty followed the system of paternal affinity 周道尊尊."

Following the system of maternal affinity of the Yin dynasty, when the king passed away, his brother, not his son, was designated as the descendant. Following the system of the paternal affinity of the Zhou dynasty, when the king passed away, his eldest son, not his brother, was designated as the descendant. According to the system of maternal affinity, when the prince passed away, his brother was acknowledged as his descendant, not his son; but given the paternal affinity of the Zhou dynasty, the eldest grandson was designated as the descendant, not his brother. Now we understand that the Yin system followed the maternal lineage, so the I Ching of the Yin dynasty followed the maternal lineage. Thus, the I Ching of the Yin dynasty set up the maternal Kun as the first hexagram; since the Zhou dynasty followed the paternal line, then the I Ching of the Zhou dynasty set up the paternal Qian as the first hexagram of the book.

Consequently, Zhou I made Qian first and Kun second in the sequence of the hexagrams, reflecting their thinking that the king is superior to his subjects, the father is superior to his sons, and the husband is superior to his wives.

Then, we are able to understand the essence of the second hexagram Kun.

Tao of Earth

The Commentary of the Symbol of the second hexagram Kun says,

> *Earth's nature is submissive.*
> *In correspondence with this*
> *The superior person enriches his virtue*
> *To sustain all beings.*

When I first worked on *The Complete I Ching* fifteen years ago, I translated the first line of Kun as, "Earth's nature is to extend and respond." Later on, I found that the ancient meaning of Kun is "submissive." The eighth wing, Discussing of the Trigrams also says, "Kun, the Earth, is submissive." On this account, the proper translation should be "Earth's nature is submissive."

Regarding Kun's beauty, the Wen Yan says:

1.
Kun is most soft;
Yet in action it is firm.
It is most still,
Yet; in nature, square.
Through following, she (he) obtains her (his) lord,
Yet still remaining her (his) nature, and thus endures.
She (he) sustains all beings
And is brilliant in transforming.

This is the way of Kun – How docile she (he) is,
Bearing Heaven and moving with time!

2.
"Straight" indicates correctness.
"Square" indicates righteousness.
The superior person respects herself (himself)
In keeping her (his) inner life straight.
And rectifies herself (himself)
In making her (his) outer action square.
When respecting and rectifying are established,
Then fulfillment of virtue will be free from isolation.
"Straight, square, and great,
Not from learning.
Nothing is unfavorable."
It shows she (he) has no doubt in what she (he) does.

3.

Although yin possesses beauty,
It is concealed,
Engaging in a king's service,
Claiming no credit for herself (himself).
This is the Tao of Earth,
The Tao of a wife,
And the Tao of one, who serves the king.
The Tao of Earth is to make no claim on her (his) own,
But to bring everything to completion.

4.

Changing and transforming of Heaven and Earth
Bring forth all plants flourishing.
If Heaven and Earth restrain their function,
Then an able person would withdraw from the light.
The I says, "Tie up a bag. No fault, no praise."
It counsels caution.

5.

A superior person should hold the quality of Earth –
Yellow is central and moderate,
Understanding and considerate.
Correcting her (his) position and perfecting her (his) action,
Her (his) beauty lies within.
It permeates her (his) whole being
And manifests in all her (his) doing.
This reveals the perfection of beauty.

6.

When yin competes against yang,
A contest is certain.
Since no yang is considered;

Then a dragon is mentioned.
Since no category is changed;
Then blood – a symbol of yin – is noted.
Blue and yellow is Heaven and Earth in fusion.
Heaven is blue, Earth yellow.

The Commentary is divided into two sections. In the first section, Confucius expounds further upon King Wen's Decision. In the second section, he provides a more detailed explanation of the Duke of Zhou's Yao Text. Both sections are based upon the moral principles of the Confucian school regarding Qian as the gua for the king, and Kun as the gua for the queen, or minister and subordinates. Qian reveals the truth of how to be a leader; Kun reveals the truth of how to be a follower. Confucian scholars consider that both leading and following should be learned and practiced.

At the beginning of this section, Confucius gives an excellent example of the Chinese dialectical point of view.

Kun is soft, yet still firm. It is still, yet also square.

Soft and firm, still and square are entirely opposite, yet in the Chinese mind they can be united. Thus Confucius says, *"Through following, she obtains her lord; yet still maintains her nature."* This is a typical Chinese dialectic – being submissive but not slavish; being independent but not rebellious. On the other hand, being a leader but not being dictatorial.

This dialectical point of view – the merging of opposites – is deeply rooted in Chinese culture. I Ching expounds first the Tian Tao 天道, the Tao of Heaven, the Di Tao 地道, the Tao of Earth, and then Ren Tao 人道, the Tao of Humanity. It instructs people that Heaven is the initiator and Earth should follow the Tao of Heaven, and humans should follow the Tao of Earth. The fourth gua, Childhood, represents the Tao of Humanity. Because King Wen had these ideas, he arranged the sequence of the I Ching putting Qian in the first place and Kun in the second place. Moreover, King Wen put Childhood in the fourth place, after the Beginning in the third place. King Wen says in the Beginning: "It is not I who seek the ignorant; the ignorant seeks me . . ." Confucius highly admired the culture of the Zhou dynasty. He said, "How brilliant is the culture of Zhou. I prefer to follow Zhou."

Confucius expounded on this subject to explain the law of cause and effect. Through the influence of the I Ching, the idea of retribution was deeply impressed into Chinese culture. The Chinese people believe that the law of cause and effect operates not only within one generation, but also through at least three generations, affecting their ancestors, themselves and their descendants. The Wen Yan on the second gua says:

> *The family that heaps goodness upon goodness*
> *Is sure to have an abundance of blessings.*
> *The family that piles evil upon evil*
> *Is sure to have an abundance of misery.*

> *Murder of a ruler by his minister,*
> *Or a father by his son,*
> *Does not result from a single day and night.*
> *Its causes have accumulated bit by bit*
> *Through the absence of early discrimination.*

> *The I says, "Treading on hoarfrost, solid ice will come."*
> *It shows the natural sequence of cause and effect.*

For this reason, the Chinese revered their ancestors after they passed away and emphasized their words, deeds and family teachings. On this account, the Chinese believe that the effects of their deeds, whether good or bad, if not fulfilled in the present life, definitely come to fruition in the life of the next generation. Thus they say, "Care only for plowing and weeding, ask not for the harvest." Bearing this in mind, Liu Bei 刘备, the emperor of the Shu Han dynasty 蜀汉, (221 A.D. – 265 A.D.), instructed his son on his deathbed, "Don't restrain your good deed because it is too tiny; don't perform your evil act because it is so little."

Both Confucianism and Taoism originated from the philosophy of the I Ching. They both followed the Tao of Earth, but they diverged. For instance, Confucius took no credit for success, but instead focused on bringing everything to completion; yet this principle was carried out more thoroughly by the Taoists. In Chinese history, the greatest prime minister was a Taoist sage named Chang Liang 张良. Chang Liang assisted the first emperor of the Han dynasty (206 B.C. – 220 A.D.), Liu Bong 刘邦, who overthrew the tyrant emperor of the Qin dynasty 秦代 (221 B.C. – 206 B.C.). Chang Liang then withdrew from active life and became a hermit.

Where did he go? No one knows.

This is the true spirit of taking no credit for success, but bringing everything to completion. Chang Liang followed the instruction of this yao: "After succeeding, resign." He embraced the Tao of I: "When things reach the extreme, they alternate to the opposite." Chang Liang realized that with success his prestige was at its highest, just short of the emperor's; but soon or later, he would fall. As he predicted, later on, the emperor became suspicious and after a time had all the other ministers killed one by one. Chang Liang has come to be regarded as the wisest person ever known in China.

When Confucius was young, he was so determined to carry out the Zhou dynasty's brilliant social system in what was a disorderly era, that even in his dreams he saw the Duke of Zhou. He encouraged his students by saying, "Having completed one's learning, one should apply oneself to being an officer." Once he told his students, "One's burden is heavy and one's course is long . . . only with death does the course stop. – Is it long?" He visited the lords of six states, trying to persuade them to participate in benevolent governing, like the Zhou system. After being rejected, he wept in grief. At the time, he did not understand that in his early days he had made many mistakes due to his inexperience and misunderstandings.

Confucius began to study the I Ching when he was fifty years old. He studied so hard that the leather thongs, which bound the bamboo tablets of his I Ching, wore out three times. At seventy years of age he said, "If some years were added to my life, I would dedicate fifty years to study of The Book of I, and then I might come to be without great fault." His attitude had changed entirely. He realized that in his early days he had made many mistakes.

The Essence of the Mare's Steadfastness

The Decision of Kun says,

> Responding.
> Sublimely prosperous and smooth,
> Favorable with a mare's steadfastness.
> Superior person has somewhere to go –
> Predetermining; he loses.
> Following; obtain a master.
> Be composed and content.
> Being steadfast and upright –
> Good fortune

Following; obtain a master

Following Chinese custom, the ancient written language had no punctuation. Depending on how one interpreted the punctuation of a clause or a sentence, different meanings appeared. Thus, different scholars have different understandings and different interpretations of the I Ching.

In terms of my understanding, to be an I Ching student, first of all, one should closely follow what The Commentary on the Symbol of the first and second hexagrams, Qian and Kun, say:

> *Keeping oneself vital without ceasing;*
> *And enrich one's virtue to sustain all beings.*

I believe everyone has a deity, no matter if he is a Muslim, a Buddhist, a Taoist, a Catholic, a Christian, or a follower of Heaven . . . No matter what one calls one's deity, one should accept the idea of "Predetermining; loses. Following; obtain a master."

As a Chinese, Heaven is my deity. In everything that I do, I follow Heaven's will. As soon as I follow Heaven's will, I feel I am all right and safe. Alternatively, if I follow my own will, I feel uncertain and lost. For instance, during the eight years of Japanese Occupation in 1937 – 1945 and after Communists took over China in 1949, especially through my experiences of twenty-two years confinement in the Communist labor camp and in the Communist prison being sentenced to death . . . the situation was awfully dangerous. A list of 120 people to be executed had been posted, and my name was second on the list; we were to be taken to the execution ground and shot. However, under my deity's guidance I felt peaceful, secure and safe. No matter how disastrous the situation was, in the end the danger always turned to safety.

Since I was thirty years old I have learned how to rely on my deity to live a life of following Heaven's will. Every night before sleep, I "install" the things I would do the next day into my mind. After a night's sound sleep, I awake in the morning clear about what to do and how to do it. Even in the case of what to write, I always seek for the Divine's guidance during my sleep or quiet times.

It seems like a miracle to me that, after suffering for so many years, by following Heaven's will, although I am ninety-three years old now, I am sound and still able to write. I have relied on following the principles of: "keeping myself vital without ceasing, and enriching my virtue to sustain all beings," as well as: "Predetermining; he loses; Following, obtain a master."

7

元 亨 利 贞

Yuan Heng Li Zhen

Yuan, heng, li, zhen 元 亨 利 贞 comprise the Decision of the first hexagram. It seems brief, only four Chinese characters, yet its connotations are profound. It serves as the foundation of all the Decisions. One scholar, Ma Qi-chang 马其昶 (1855 – 1930), said: "Actually it is the guiding principle of the whole book."

Decision, in Chinese, is tuan 彖. Tuan 彖 is the word associated with the symbol of the gua explaining its significance. Originally, tuan 彖 was a fierce animal with sharp teeth for cutting. The ancients used it to represent a resolute decision. King Wen tried to employ the least words, rich in content but succinct in style, to summarize the substance of the gua. On many occasions, the words of the Decision employ images to explain the significance of the gua. For instance, the Decision of the second gua, Responding, is "Sublimely prosperous and smooth. Favorable with a mare's steadfastness." It employs the image of a female horse to convey steadfastness. On the contrary, the Decision of the first gua, Initiating, is simply "sublime and initiating 元; prosperous and smooth 亨; harmonious and beneficial 利; steadfast and upright 贞." It does not employ any images and is abstract in nature.

In fact, it does not require images to express the first gua's meaning. The Decision of the first gua does not comment on the appearance of Heaven, but instead describes its functions. The functions of Heaven can be summarized in one word – vitality. "Vitality" reveals the constant rotating and movement of the celestial body, which one can neither stop nor change its trajectory. The ancients employed the four Chinese characters yuan, heng, li and zhen to explain it. When these four characters are integrated, they become yuan 元 itself. Then yuan is *vitality*. When yuan is differentiated, it becomes yuan 元, heng 亨, li 利 and zhen 贞. The ancients explained yuan, heng, li and zhen as spring, summer, autumn and winter. They also described them as sprouting, growing, blooming and fruiting. As Confucius says, "Does Heaven speak? The four seasons follow their courses, and all beings are continually being produced, but Heaven doesn't say anything!"

Tao of Heaven as well as the Tao of Humanity

In *The Complete I Ching* I translated:

> Yuan as sublime and initiating;
> Heng as prosperous and smooth;
> Li as favorable and beneficial;
> Zhen as steadfast and upright.

Yuan, heng, li and zhen represent the Tao of Heaven 天道, as well as the Tao of Humanity 人道. As the Tao of Heaven, they are spring, summer, autumn and winter; or originating, developing, maturing and declining. The four characters, as a whole, signify vitality and persistence, which encourages people to keep their spirits vital and unrelenting.

As the Tao of Humanity, Wen Yan 文言, The Commentary on the Words of the Text says:

> *Yuan 元, sublime and initiating,*
> *It is the first and chief quality of all goodness.*
> *Heng 亨, prosperous and smooth,*

It is the accumulation of all excellence.
Li 利, favorable and beneficial,
It is the harmony of all that is just.
Zhen 贞, the steadfast and upright,
It is the essence of all actions.

In the beginning, yuan, heng, li and zhen were easy to understand. Some 200 years after the Zhou dynasty 周代, in the Spring and Autumn Period 春秋 (770 – 476 B.C.), they needed further explanation. The above explanation in Wen Yan are the words that Confucius used to reinforce what Mu Jiang 穆姜 had said. Afterward, once Confucius wrote the Wen Yan, people could not understand what Mu Jiang had explained; then commentaries and sub-commentaries came out one after another.

Up to and including the present time, most Chinese I Ching scholars have agreed that yuan, heng, li and zhen are the guiding principles of the I Ching. Yuan, heng, li and zhen contain the Tao of Heaven, as well as the Tao of Humanity. What the Wen Yan stresses is employing the Tao of Humanity to explain yuan, heng, li and zhen.

Zi Xia 子夏, one of the favorite students of Confucius, believed that yuan is beginning; heng is open; li is harmony; and zhen is upright.

The Wen Yan explains that yuan is the highest virtue, the ultimate of all goodness. In other words, all goodness comes from yuan 元, and yuan 元 comes from benevolence 仁. Benevolence includes kindheartedness, generosity and compassion.

Dong Zhong-shu 董仲舒 (179 B.C.– 104 B.C.) the most eminent philosopher of the West Han dynasty, not only accepted the unity of Heaven and Humanity 天人合一, but went a step further advocating the induction of Heaven and Humanity 天人感应. He stressed that, "the king as well as the nobilities should all practice the five constant virtues 五常." The five constant virtues are benevolence 仁, righteousness 义, propriety 礼, wisdom 智 and fidelity 信. Afterward, many scholars thought that yuan 元 should be benevolence 仁, heng 亨 should be propriety 礼, li 利 should be righteousness 义 and zhen 贞 should be fidelity 信.

Shao Yong 邵雍 (1011 A.D. – 1077 A.D.) an eminent scholar of his time, said, "Since Heaven changes and human beings follow; then yuan, heng, li and zhen become the 'changes' of I. When human beings act and Heaven responds; then good fortune 吉, misfortune 凶, humiliation 吝 and regret 悔 come into existence. Good fortune, misfortune, humiliation, and regret are 'responses' to the various behaviors of human beings."

The Essence of the I Ching

The essence of the I Ching is yuan 元.

Yuan 元 unites heng 亨, li 利 and zhen 贞. When the four virtues are integrated, it is yuan 元; while differentiated, they become yuan 元, heng 亨, li 利 and zhen 贞. Thus, The Commentary 象传 says, "Great indeed is the greatness of Initiating 乾, to which all beings owe their beginning." "Perfect indeed is the greatness of Responding 坤, to which all beings owe their birth." As yuan 元 is the genesis of all beings, all beings owe their beginning and birth to it.

Therefore, what the I Ching teaches people is to produce, develop and maintain the quality of yuan 元. Thus, the ancients considered that yuan was the highest and most perfect virtue. Through thousands of years, it became the virtue that "superior persons 君子" should possess. A superior person 君子 is a person of integrity. According to the Confucian school, yuan 元 is benevolence 仁. Benevolence includes kindness, generosity and compassion. The Chinese character of benevolence 仁 is composed by combining two characters – the first is "two 二" and the other is "person 人"; which reflects that, where there are two persons, there should be benevolence. Benevolence can be summarized by what Confucius says, "What you do not want others to do to yourself, do not do it to others 己所不欲勿施于人."

Dong Zhong-shu 董仲舒, the greatest scholar of the West Han dynasty (206 B.C.– 771 B.C.) said, "Those who uphold justice, never give a thought to profit 正其宜不谋其利"; also, "Those who understand the Tao, never give a thought to merit 明其道不计其功."

Deeply influenced by all these thoughts from the Confucian school, I believe that the essence of the I Ching is: "To make man a man 人其人"; or "To educate a man to be a man 人化."

Seven Hexagrams Bear the Decision of Yuan, Heng, Li, Zhen

Among the sixty-four hexagrams there are seven that include yuan 元, heng 亨, li 利 and zhen 贞 in the text of their Decisions. These four Chinese characters comprise the Decision of the first gua, Initiating. However, when these characters appear in the Decisions of the other six above-mentioned gua, the Chinese characters appear with modifiers. Besides Initiating 乾 (1), the gua containing yuan 元, heng 亨, li 利 and zhen 贞 in their Decisions are Responding 坤 (2), Beginning 屯 (3), Following 随 (17), Approaching 临 (19), Without Falsehood 无妄 (25), and Abolishing the Old 革 (49).

With respect to Initiating 乾, the first gua; yuan, heng, li and zhen represent the Tao of Heaven. These four characters supplement and complement each other as a single merit, carrying the firmness of the yang 阳. They are the creative power to create the myriad beings. They bear the meaning of initiating, growing, accomplishing and fulfilling.

With respect to Responding 坤 (2), yuan, heng, li and zhen represent the Tao of Earth. In this case, these four characters represent the virtues of gentleness and submission of the yin 阴. Besides, the Earth holds the promise of producing and bringing the myriad beings into existence. As Initiating and Responding represent the Tao of Heaven and the Tao of Earth, Initiating is the principal and Responding is the subordinate. Responding obeys and follows Initiating.

The other five hexagrams that have Decisions including yuan, heng, li and zhen are Beginning 屯 (3), Following 随 (17), Approaching 临 (19), Without Falsehood 无妄 (25) and Abolishing the Old 革 (49). Yuan – heng 元亨 is "great smooth and prosperous", li – zhen 利贞 is "beneficial to be righteous and steadfast."

Moreover, each of these five gua has its own distinguishing feature. For instance, Beginning 屯 bears the significance of "just starting"; Following 随 bears the significance of "going after"; "Approaching 临 bears the significance of "becoming great"; Without Falsehood 无妄 bears the significance of "greatest sincerity"; Abolishing the Old 革 bears the significance of "making huge changes." Assuming all these attributes *in each case* are carried out with "righteousness and steadfastness," the outcome will be "prosperous and smooth."

Initiating Signifying Initial and Vital

The Decision of Initiating says,

> Sublime and initiating 元.
> Prosperous and smooth 亨.
> Harmonious and beneficial 利.
> Steadfast and upright 贞.

It denotes the four essential qualities of a king (in ancient times) or of a leader (in present times).

Qian 乾, Initiating ䷀, is Heaven ☰ above, and Heaven ☰ below. All six lines are yang elements. It is a gua demonstrating how an emperor or a leader should be.

In this gua, the four Chinese characters yuan 元, heng 亨, li 利 and zhen 贞 represent the four essential qualities of a leader. Yuan 元 is initiating. Heng 亨 is smoothly progressing. Li 利, in ancient times, was harmony. It was absolutely not seeking personal gain, as now most people think; instead, it was pursuing mutual benefit. In pursuing mutual benefit, there should be harmony amongst all those involved. Zhen 贞 represents making unremitting efforts.

元 Yuan is creating. It manifests something from nothing; from little to big; from weak to strong, from starting to ending . . . In every period of time, a leader is thus able to realize his resourceful ability.

亨 Heng is leading, going smoothly without blockages. It is the quality of a leader being sensible and reasonable. A leader is able to hold a practical view and demonstrate good sense. It is the ability of carrying out and fulfilling the original goal.

利 Li is harmony. It is the capability of a leader to unify the will of all who are working under him. If everyone in a group is able to experience his value and is doing his best, then all obstacles can be overcome.

贞 Zhen is loyalty and constancy. It is the loyalty and constancy of one's original intention. No matter what kind of intention one has, as long as one is able to persist with it, it will be fulfilled.

Responding Signifies Gentleness and Obedience

The Decision of Responding says,

> Sublimely prosperous and smooth 元亨.
> Favorable with a mare's steadfastness 利牝马之贞.
> Superior person has somewhere to go 君子有攸往.
> Predetermining; he will lose 先迷.
> Following; obtain a master 后得主.
> Favorable in the southwest: get friends 利西南得朋.
> In the northeast: Lose friends 东北丧朋.
> Be composed and content 安.
> Being steadfast and upright: good fortune 贞吉.

There are twenty-nine Chinese characters in the Decision; it is twenty-five characters more than yuan, heng, li and zhen. It reminds people that, as a human being one should follow the will of Heaven. If "pre-determined," thinking and acting with his own intention, he will lose. Only by following the Divine's instruction will one be led and guided.

The Decision of Responding says, "Favorable with a mare's steadfastness 利牝马之贞." A female horse is gentle and submissive but vital in carrying a heavy load or running fast. Responding reflects the virtue of the Earth. It is obeying an order and complying with a master's instruction. As Responding is subordinate, Responding ranks as secondary. Therefore, yin following yang is the right course. If the yin pre-determines, all will be lost.

Beginning Signifies Hardship at the Beginning

The Decision of Beginning 屯 says,

> Sublimely prosperous and smooth 元亨.
> Favorable to be steadfast and upright 利贞.
> Do not act 勿用.
> There is somewhere to go 有攸往.
> Favorable to establish feudal lords 利建侯.

There are twelve Chinese characters in the Decision. It is eight Chinese characters more than yuan, heng, li and zhen. It reminds people in this time-situation that one should not move forward rashly.

This is an auspicious gua. It expounds the truth that in a newly established situation there is plenty of potential to develop. On the other hand, it also contains latent difficulty.

The name of the gua 屯 brings to mind a tiny sprout shooting out of the ground. Most people think sprouts are growing only in the spring; but the ancient Chinese realized that there was a life force latent in the seed throughout the winter. The ancients perceived the difficulties of a plant emerging from the ground. The little plant must overcome the tremendous pressure of the soil. There must be a wholehearted willingness to grow. Thus, the gua is bestowed with the four outstanding qualities of yuan, heng, li and zhen as with the first and the second gua. Only seven out of the sixty-four gua in the *I Ching* possess these four qualities.

The structure of the gua is Cloud ☵ over Thunder ☳. It presents a vivid picture of a tremendous power, represented by thunder, lying at the base of the clouds.

The Commentary on the Decision says,

Beginning
The firm and the yielding united at the very beginning.
Difficulties come into being.

Movement in the midst of danger,
Great prosperity and smoothness come
Through steadfastness and uprightness.

The action of thunder and rain
Filled things up everywhere.
At the beginning of creation,

There was irregularity and disorder.
It was favorable to establish feudal lords
But unstable conditions still might arise.

This is the Chinese concept of genesis. Before Heaven and Earth existed, there was nothing – void. During creation, clouds, rain and thunder appeared together. There was irregularity and disorder. After the world was brought into being – regularity and order were gradually established. Based on the concept of the union of yin and yang, Chinese scholars came to employ "Cloud and Rain 云雨" to suggest the actions of lovemaking.

After human beings came into being, there began an entirely new phase. The Tao of Humanity had gradually been established; and the concept of the time-honored unity of Heaven and Humanity gradually was founded and accepted.

It was favorable to establish feudal lords in this time-situation. In present times, the equivalent would be to form co-operational team-working forces. However, unstable conditions might arise.

Following Signifies How to Influence People to Follow

The Decision of Following 随 says:

> Sublimely prosperous and smooth 元亨.
> Favorable to be steadfast and upright 利贞.
> No fault 无咎.

There are six Chinese characters in the Decision. There are two Chinese characters more than yuan, heng, li and zhen. It reminds people that only by behaving humbly can one entice others to follow. If one wants to lead, one must first learn to be led.

The structure of the gua is Lake ☱ above, Thunder ☳ below. Two yang elements underneath a yin element form the image of Lake. One yang element underneath two yin elements forms the image of Thunder. It demonstrates that the strong allows itself to follow the weak. Moreover, the attribute of Lake is joy and that of Thunder is movement. Only by behaving humbly and joy-fully can one make others follow. If one wants to lead, one must first learn to be led. In this way, there will be progress and success.

This gua is special, it expounds the way to influence people to follow. In human society, conflicts are unavoidable. Occasionally one has to give up one's own interest or ideas to harmonize with others. This is the way to maintain harmony and delight in a community.

Approaching Signifies Toward Greatness

The Decision of Approaching 临 says,

> Sublimely prosperous and smooth 元亨.
> Favorable to be steadfast and upright 利贞.
> As in the eighth month 至于八月.
> Misfortune comes 有凶.

There are ten Chinese characters in the Decision. It is six Chinese characters more than yuan, heng, li and zhen. It reminds people that during a time of great expansion one should not wait and see, but participate positively in the event sincerely and wisely. On the other hand, be aware of the waxing and waning of the yin and the yang, stop before going too far.

The name of the gua, Approaching, does not contain the attribute of "toward greatness"; but the image of the gua ䷒ shows that the two yang elements are expanding. It gives a hint that in this time-situation, the way of "superior persons" is expanding, and the way of "inferior persons" is shrinking. "Superior person" in I Ching denotes "a man of worth," and "inferior persons" denotes "men of vile character." As Confucius says, "What the superior man seeks, is in himself; what the inferior person seeks, is in others. 君子求诸己, 小人求诸人."

The Commentary on the Decision says,

> *Approaching.*
> *The firm is advancing and growing.*
> *Joyous and obedient.*
> *Being central and properly corresponded to.*
> *Great success along with his correctness.*
> *This is the Tao of Heaven.*
> *At the end of eighth month,*

There will be misfortune.
Remission is not too long in coming.

A leader, especially a minister leading a government, should influence people joyfully and obediently with noble character and appropriate conduct. He never would employ flattery and deception to attract people to follow him. He should obtain great success along with his correctness. Once a student, Zi Lu 子路, asked about government 问政. Confucius said 子曰, "Go before the people with your example, and work tirelessly in their best interest "先之, 劳之." Zi Lu requested further instruction 请益, and was answered, 曰, "Be not weary in these things! 无倦."

The Commentary on the Decision says that the yang element as a minister at the second place is central, and properly corresponding to the yin element at the fifth place. It demonstrates that the king and the minister are taking concerted action. Joyfully and obediently as the firm is advancing; he is following the Tao of Heaven.

As one who is following the Tao of Heaven, one should not neglect the law of "Things go into reverse when pushed to the extremity. 物极必反." So the Decision reminds, "As to the eight month; misfortune comes."

Without Falsehood Signifies Utmost Truthfulness

The Decision of Without Falsehood 无妄 says,

> Sublimely prosperous and smooth 元亨.
> Favorable to be steadfast and upright 利贞.
> If one's intention is not truthful 其匪正.
> There is trouble 有眚.
> Unfavorable to have somewhere to go 不利有攸往.

There are fourteen Chinese characters in the Decision. It is ten Chinese characters more than yuan, heng, li and zhen. The name of the gua, in Chinese, is Wu Wang 无妄, Without Falsehood. It reminds people that one should not be untruthful, dishonest or insincere. If one's intention is not truthful, but instead dishonest and insincere, there is trouble. It will be unfavorable to have somewhere to go.

The image of the gua is Heaven ☰ above, Thunder ☳ below.

Heaven ☰ bears yuan, heng, li and zhen, the four merits; and Thunder ☳ moves in accord with the Tao of Heaven. Thus, this is an auspicious gua.

If Thunder moves in accord with a human's intention, and the human's intention is not truthful, there is trouble.

This gua displays the wisdom of holding to the truth. No matter how situations change, truthfulness should never change. Ancient Chinese did not have a personal God; they submitted to the will of Heaven and resigned themselves to their fate. They believed that to live and to act in harmony with the will of Heaven were the nature and the duty of humanity. To act in accord with the virtue of Heaven would eventually bring everlasting fortune and success. If one had this faith, then one was able to not count on the harvest while plowing. This attitude does not neglect the law of cause and effect. What is important is whether one's attitude and motivation are aligned with the virtue of Heaven. What is considered first is not the reward one will attain, but instead whether the work is really good for humanity.

Abolishing the Old Signifies a Revolution

The Decision of Abolishing the Old 革 says,

> Proper day 已日
> Obtained confidence from people 乃孚.
> Supremely prosperous and smooth 元亨.
> Favorable to be steadfast and upright 利贞.
> Regret vanishes 悔亡.

There are ten Chinese characters in the Decision. It is six Chinese characters more than yuan, heng, li and zhen. The aim of abolishing the old is to establish the new. It reminds people that the timing and the motivation of a revolution are crucially important.

The gua preceding this gua, Abolishing the Old, is Replenishing.

The Sequence of the Gua says, "The silt at the bottom of the well needs to be removed. Thus, after Replenishing, Abolishing the Old follows."

The Decision of Replenishing says, "The site of a village may be moved, not the well." People, "coming and going," "drawing, drawing," the water "neither loses nor gains." It suggests that a government should serve the people with no self-interests.

In the first line, the Duke of Zhou describes the condition of the well – the government – the well is "too old"; "there is silt." Thus, "No people come to drink the water, not even the birds." In the second line he says, in the bottom of the well there are only tiny carp, and the bucket is leaking. It gives a hint that the system of the government is of no use at all; it only damages peoples' lives. In the third line, the Duke of Zhou says, "The well is dredged," "still no people come." Then, in the fourth and fifth lines he explains that the well is tiled, and the water is icy pure. Then people come again. At the top line he says, "The well is fully drawn," and suggests, "Do not cover!" . . . All these give hint that the system of the government is too old, which needs changing. Otherwise, the newly established system has deceived the people, becoming tyrannical and degenerate, even trading profit for the best interests of people. Each of these governments opposes the will of Heaven and is against the wishes of the people. The old system needs to be abolished and the new one should be established.

The Commentary on the Decision says,

> *Proper day.*
> *Upon it obtains confidence from people.*
> *When the revolutionary tempest breaks out,*
> *Faith will accord with it.*

> *Heaven and Earth abolish the old and bring about the new.*
> *Then the four seasons complete their changes.*
> *Tong and Wu abolished the old and brought about the new.*
> *They obeyed the will of Heaven*
> *And in accord the wishes of people.*
> *The time and meaning of abolishing the old is truly great!*

In the course of ancient Chinese history, there were two most significant revolutions. One was the rebellion led by King Tang who overthrew the tyrant of Jie of the Xia dynasty and established the Shang dynasty. The other was the revolution led by King Wu, son of King Wen, who overthrew the tyrant of Shang and established the Zhou dynasty. The Chinese believed that both revolutions carried out the will of Heaven and realized the wishes of the people.

Mencius says,

> The son of Heaven receives instruction from Heaven and becomes King. Whether there is instruction from Heaven depends on the wishes of people.
> Those who oppose the wishes of people oppose the will of Heaven.
> It is certain that they will be abolished by the new one authorized by Heaven.

According to history, before King Wu initiated the revolution, he reformed the old social system in his domain by abolishing slavery. In this way he replenished his people and strengthened his territory. In the thirty-four gua of the Lower Canon, only this gua is bestowed with the most auspicious blessing of yuan, heng, li and zhen. People had confidence in the overthrow of the old system. Thus, all regret vanished and a new era began.

All these are the sources of Chinese civilization. There is always *hope* for the future.

On the other hand, the Chinese have tremendous patience to wait for a better situation. They believe deeply what the I Ching teaches – "Things developing to the extreme, a dramatic change to the opposite will come." They are preparing and waiting for the right time, the suitable situation, the appropriate leadership, and the unexpected incident, which will ignite the fuse.

8

易 经 的 断 语

The Judgment of the I Ching

At the beginning, I Ching was a manual of divination. Later on, it came to be regarded as a handbook of proper behavior.

In ancient times, for decisions related to moving a capital or sending an army, as well as in considering a marriage or managing a burial . . . the ancients would consult the Divine through use of the I Ching. After King Wen composed the I Ching, especially after Confucius wrote The Commentaries – The Eight Wings, gradually people changed their minds and considered I Ching primarily as a handbook to guide appropriate behavior.

There are 64 gua and 384 yao in I Ching. The Decision of a gua indicates the potential of a particular time-situation; it provides guidance to people on how to act properly to create good fortune and avoid misfortune.

In this way, I Ching reveals how everyone's fate relies on one's own actions.

Judgments in the I Ching
There are six judgments in the I Ching; they are ji 吉, xiong 凶, hui 悔, lin 吝, li 厉 and jiu 咎. These judgments can be grouped into two categories, either good fortune or misfortune. There are over five-hundred occurrences of such

judgments, occupying one-fourth of the text of the book. Each yao 爻 possesses at least one of these judgments.

Ji 吉 is good fortune; xiong 凶 is misfortune. The rest of the judgments – hui 悔, lin 吝, li 厉 and jiu 咎 – state different levels of misfortune. Contemplating these six items, the ancients realized that the nature and appearance of misfortune are subtle and wide-ranging. Thus, Confucius advises: "Think thrice before you act 三思而行!"

The ancient Chinese believed that one created one's own reality. Only when the instructions of the I Ching were followed could the possibility of getting good fortune or avoiding misfortune be accomplished. These instructions are not the dross, but the essence of the I Ching, which enables the philosophy of the I Ching to be applied in a practical manner.

The Great Treatise says,

> *The ancient sages established gua,*
> *So their symbols can be perceived.*
> *They appended the fastening text.*
> *So that good fortune and misfortune can be determined.*
>
> *As the firm and the yielding lines evolve*
> *And displace one another,*
> *Changes and transformations come forth.*
>
> *Therefore good fortune and misfortune*
> *Are symbols of gain and loss.*
> *Regret and humiliation*
> *Are signs of anxiety and guilt.*
>
> *Changes and transformations*
> *Are signs of progress and retreat.*
> *The firm and the yielding*
> *Are symbols of brightness and darkness.*

Professor Zhou Shan 周山 created statistics on the occurrences of the judgments in the Decisions as well as in the Yao Text. There are over ninety occurrences of xiong 凶, lin 吝, hui 悔, li 厉 and jiu 咎; and over two hundred occurrences of ji 吉, li 利 and no fault 无咎. Judgments stating good fortune are two times more frequent than those of misfortune. Among misfortune judgments, there are also occurrences of transforming misfortune to good fortune. Clearly, Zhou I 周易 is not a book of grief and sorrow, as some I Ching books have suggested. It is a book encouraging people to work hard for success and prosperity.

The Positions of Yao 爻位

Each gua has six yao. Analyzing the position of the yao is one of the keys to understanding its meaning.

Each of the six lines of a gua has a name. First, the ancients named the yin element as "Six" and the yang element as "Nine." Then, the yin element at the bottom position was called "Initial Six 初六," the yang element at the bottom position was called "Initial Nine 初九." The yin element at the second position was called "Six Second 六二" and the yang element at the second position was called "Nine Second 九二." The yin element at the third position was called "Six Third 六三," and the yang element at the third position was called "Nine Third 九三." The yin element at the fourth position was called "Six Fourth 六四," and the yang element at the fourth position was called "Nine Fourth 九四." The yin element at the fifth position was called "Six Fifth 六五," and the yang element at the fifth position was called "Nine Fifth 九五." The yin element at the top position was called "Top Six 上六," and the yang element at the top position was called "Top Nine 上九."

For instance, in Household ䷗ (37) the thirty-seventh gua, from the bottom up the yao are Initial Nine 初九, Six Second 六二, Nine Third 九三, Six Fourth 六四, Nine Fifth 九五, and Top Nine 上九. In this way, the name of the yao embodies the quality of the yao as well as its position. Thus, Nine represents yang elements and Six represents yin elements; initial, second, third, fourth, fifth, and top represent the position of the yao.

These six positions represent six stages of the development of a thing, as well as its position, condition and status. Positions move successively from the bottom up, embodying the development of a thing or an event. For instance:

The initial position – signifies the germination stage of a thing. It indicates that one should hide and not be active.

The second position – signifies that one is beginning to show one's brilliant talents, or to display one's remarkable abilities.

The third position – signifies one's preliminary success. One should be cautious and aware of critical conditions.

The fourth position – signifies that things have developed into a new accomplishment. One should maintain a keen vigilance.

The fifth position – signifies one's complete success. One should be satisfied, and not insatiably greedy.

The top position – signifies one's final stage. One should be aware of things reaching the extremity and turning into their opposites.

Correct Position and Incorrect Position 正与不正

There are correct and incorrect positions. The Commentary on the Decisions states that there are three yin positions and three yang positions of a yao. The initial position 初位, the third position 三位, and the fifth position 五位 are yang positions; the second position 二位, the fourth position 四位, and the top position 上位 are yin positions 阳位. If any yang element occupies the yang position 阳位, it is at the correct position, a condition called "getting the position 得位." Likewise, if any yin element occupies the yin position 阴位, it is also at the correct position, and said to be "getting the position 得位."

Take a look at Already Fulfilled ䷾ (63), the sixty-third gua. In this gua, all yang elements are at the yang positions and all yin elements are at the yin positions. All these elements get the correct positions 得位. On the other hand, consider Not Yet Fulfilled ䷿ (64), the sixty-fourth gua. In this gua, all yin elements occupy yang positions and all yang elements occupy yin positions. Thus all the elements are "getting the incorrect positions 失位."

Generally, "getting the position 得位" signifies good fortune; and "not getting the position 失位" signifies misfortune. For instance, Innermost Sincerity ䷼ (61) the sixty-first gua, Six Third is a yin element at a yang place, the place is incorrect. The Commentary on the Symbol says, "Confronts an adversary. Now beats the drum; now leaves off. Now sobs, now sings. The place is not appropriate." On the other hand, the Nine Fifth is a yang element at a yang position; it is "getting the correct position 得位." The Yao Text says, "Innermost sincerity linked with another hand in hand. His place is correct and appropriate."

When an element gets "the proper place 得位" it stands for things developing on a right course, or according to a regular pattern. On the other hand, when an element gets "an incorrect position 失位," it signifies deviating from the right way or running counter to the regular pattern.

However, "getting the correct position 得位" or "getting the incorrect position 失位" is not the absolute standard to judge good fortune or misfortune, advantage or disadvantage. The standard of judgment might be influenced by other considerations.

Central or Not Central 中与不中

"Central" means "central position 中位." Each of the sixty-four gua has two central positions, namely the second position 二位 and the fifth position 五位. The second position is the central position in the lower gua 下卦; and the fifth position is the central position in the upper gua 上卦. "Central position 中位" signifies that things or situations are strictly impartial and just.

Being Central 中 Is Superior to Being Correct 正

The Commentary on the Symbol holds the idea that, generally speaking, although a yao gets "an incorrect position 失正 or 失位," if it occupies a "central position 得中" it would result in good fortune.

The Great Commentary says, "The second position gets more praise; and the fifth position, more merit." For instance, Eradicating ䷗ (21), the twenty-first gua, in which Six Fifth gets "an incorrect position 失正" but is situated in a "central position 得中." Thus, The Commentary on the Decision says,

"Although the place is not appropriate, it is still favorable to administer justice." In Not Yet Fulfilled ䷿ (64) the sixty-fourth gua, all six yao get "incorrect positions 失正"; but The Commentary on the Decision says, "At the beginning, good fortune; for the yielding is in the central." It is because the yin element in the fifth position is at a "central position." The "good fortune" of the second yao is explained by The Commentary on the Symbol, "Good fortune for the Second Nine, it is correct and in accord with proper actions."

Central as well as Correct 中正

Among the sixty-four gua, there are some in which the yin element occupies the second position and the yang element occupies the fifth position, as is the case with Hindrance ䷋ (12), the twelfth gua. In Chinese, both central and correct are called "zhong zhen 中正." It is a particularly satisfactory situation. The Commentary on the Symbol of the second yao says, "For the great person, accepting the hindrance brings progress and success." Of the fifth yao, it says, "To the superior person, good fortune. The position is appropriate."

In I Ching, "central as well as correct 中正" is even more auspicious.

Responding and Corresponding 应与正应

In each gua, among the six yao there are "responding relationships 应" between the initial yao with the fourth yao, the second yao with the fifth yao, and the third yao with the top yao. This relationship is called "responding 应."

If any two yao are "responding yao," one is yin and the other is yang, based upon the theory of "the yin and the yang mutually supporting each other 阴阳互助." This relationship is a "corresponding relationship," or simply called "corresponding 正应."

For instance, consider the last two gua, Already Fulfilled ䷾ (63) and Not Yet Fulfilled ䷿ (64). In the case of Already Fulfilled ䷾ (63), all the responding yao are complimentary, their relationships are "corresponding 正应." It is the same condition in Not Yet Fulfilled ䷿ (64).

Generally, if a yao is "corresponding with" another yao, it signals good fortune; because the yin and the yang mutually help each other.

This is a supplementary 补充 characteristic for a line that is "getting the position 当位." For instance, in Not Yet Fulfilled ䷿ (64), the sixty-fourth gua, all the six yao are in incorrect positions, but the text says: "Although all lines are not in their proper places, the firm and the yielding correspond with each other." Generally, if a yao is "corresponding with" another yao, there is good fortune; because yin and yang mutually help each other. Otherwise, there would be misfortune.

With respect to Great Harvest ䷍ (14), the fourteenth gua, the yin element situates in the fifth place. The fifth place is a yang place. Here a yin element is situated at yang place, obviously the place is "incorrect"; but the yao text says, "Sincere and truthful communication makes dignity shine through. Good fortune." Here is a yin yao at a yang place, it is in an "incorrect place." It should be misfortune. But now the text says "good fortune." Why? The Commentary on the Decision explains, "Great Harvest. The yielding obtains the honored position, great and central. The upper and the lower correspond." It is obvious that the fifth yao is a yin element at a yang place. Although it is not in the correct place, it is corresponding with the yang element in the second place. Although the place is "incorrect," it still represents "good fortune."

In I Ching, when a yin element or a yang element gets the correct position in the second place or the fifth place, they are "getting the central and right position 中正." If a yin element is at the second place and a yang element is at the fifth place, they are also "correct as well as corresponding with each other 既正且中." Some scholars call this condition "harmonizing with each other 中和." I Ching considers "harmonizing with each other 中和" as the best of all conditions.

Later on, all Confucian scholars highly regarded the relationship of "harmonizing with each other 中和" between two persons. As Confucius had said, "Superior persons harmonize with each other; even if not engaged in the same interest or in the same pursuit. 君子和而不同."

Carrying and Mounting 承与乘

In I Ching, the situation of a yao sitting on a yao immediately below it is called "mounting 乘." Each yin yao sitting on a yang yao is called "mounting on a

," which signifies a weak element overriding a strong element; or an inferior overrides a superior. The result is not good. On the other hand, when a yang yao mounts on a yin yao, it is considered "normal" and "mounting" is not mentioned. It can be seen that I Ching supports the idea that "the yang should be upheld and the yin should be restrained 扶阳抑阴."

Normally, "upholding the yang and restraining the yin" represents the principle of "upholding positive attitude against negative attitude," encouraging people to remain vital without ceasing.

But people of heretical schools take advantage of this concept, interpreting it in an incorrect way suggesting that I Ching carries the idea of "promoting the male and subordinating the female 扶男抑女." This interpretation is incorrect.

Departing 往 and Arriving 来

I Ching also considers that the upper gua and the lower gua, as well as the upper yao and the lower yao, can "move up or come down 上往下来." Moving up is "going upward from lower." Moving down is "coming downward from above." In I Ching, "going upward from lower" is called "departing 往"; "coming downward from above" is called "arriving 来." Departing and arriving relates to good fortune and misfortune.

For instance, the Decision of Advance ䷊ (11), the eleventh gua says, "The little is departing, the great is arriving." In I Ching, "the little" represents the inferior; "the great" represents the superior. Observe that the image of Heaven ☰, the great, has already arrived from above, and the image of Earth ☷, the little, has already departed from below.

The Commentary on the Decision says, "The way of the superior is expanding; the way of the inferior is shrinking." What does it means?

I Ching holds the idea that when Heaven and Earth communicate well, myriad things are smoothly and pleasantly coming into being. This time–situation is seen in Advance 泰, which the ancients considered a representation of a prosperous country with its people living in peace.

But, as Heaven is high above and the Earth is low beneath, how can they communicate? The ancients considered that their energy communicated. What the image of Advance ䷊ expresses is that the energy of Heaven has already come down from above and the energy of Earth has already gone up from below.

On the other hand, it is the opposite situation in Hindrance ☷☰ (12), the twelfth gua. The Decision of Hindrance says, "The great is departing, the little is arriving." The Commentary on the Decision explains, "The way of the little is expanding; the way of the great is shrinking."

In both cases, the Decisions link "departing" and "arriving" with "the way of the superior and the way of the inferior either expanding or shrinking."

A Brief Summary

I Ching is a book composed of sixty-four gua, and each gua is composed of six lines. Lines are its essential materials. The six lines are arranged according to the time-situation that the gua represent.

The initial line is difficult to understand, and the top line is easy to understand, for they stand in the relationship of cause and effect. The judgment on the first line is tentative, but at the top line everything has attained completion.

The second and the fourth place correspond in their work but are differentiated by their positions. They do not correspond with regard to the degree to which they have positive attributes. The second is usually praised, the fourth is usually warned against, because the fourth stands near the ruler.

The third and the fifth places correspond in their work but are differentiated by their positions. Third usually has misfortune, the fifth usually has merit, because they are graded according to rank. The weaker is endangered; the stronger has victory.

Humbleness Is Extraordinarily Unique

Among the sixty-four gua, only the fifteenth gua, Humbleness ☷☶ (15), is extraordinarily unique in that all six yao represent good fortune, no matter whether they are "central" or "correct," or not. It is clear that I Ching upholds virtue and morality. Besides being central 中, correct 正 and upright 直, one should be humble 謙.

Both Confucius and Lao Tze learned a great deal from this gua. What Confucius learned is fully expressed in his commentaries. What Lao Tze learned can be found in what he says in his Tao Te Ching:

I have three treasures
That I guard and hold dear.
The first is love.
The second is contentment.
The third is humbleness.
Only the loving are courageous;
Only the content are magnanimous;
Only the humble are capable of leading.

Humanity: Bridging Heaven and Earth

I Ching considers that there are three most significant things in the universe – Heaven, Earth and Humanity. Heaven is above on the top. Earth is below at the bottom. Humanity is positioned in the middle. The ancients regarded Humanity as the bridge between Heaven and Earth. These three things are the root of King Wen's philosophy, which becomes the central theme of the I Ching, namely the unity of Heaven and Humanity 天人合一. Thus, in each six-lined gua, the top two positions represent Heaven, the bottom two positions represent Earth, and the middle two positions represent Humanity. The spirit of Humanity can move up and descend down according to one's moral accomplishment.

As a student of the I Ching, through symbolic thinking 形象思维 one is able to learn through the relationships of the lines, thereby grasping the proper timing and the essence of a situation 时态 and understanding how to advance and how to retreat 进退, how to join and how to separate with others 离合. And most importantly, how to get Divine guidance 灵感.

Predetermining; Loses. Following; Obtain a Master

The Decision of the second gua, Responding 坤, says,

Responding.
Sublimely prosperous and smooth,
Favorable with a mare's steadfastness.
Superior person has somewhere to go –

Predetermining; loses.
Following; obtain a master.
Be composed and content.
Being steadfast and upright,
Good fortune.

According to I Ching, a human being should honor Heaven and accept Heaven as the Divine, and regard himself as a female horse serving Heaven.

The seventh wing of Wen Yan 文言 reveals what the quality of a human should be, saying:

1

Kun is most soft,
Yet in action it is firm.
It is most still,
Yet in nature, square.

Through following, she obtains her lord,
Yet still maintains her nature and thus endures.
She contains all beings
And is brilliant in transforming.

This is the way of Kun – How docile it is,
Bearing Heaven and moving with time!

2

The family that heaps goodness upon goodness
Is sure to have an abundance of blessings.
The family that piles evil upon evil
Is sure to have an abundance of misery.

Murder of a ruler by his minister,
Or a father by his son,

Does not result from a single day and night.
Its causes have accumulated bit by bit
Through the absence of early discrimination.
The I says, "Trading on hoarfrost, solid ice will come."
It shows the natural sequence of cause and effect.

"Straight" indicates correctness.
"Square" indicates righteousness.
The superior person respects herself
In keeping her inner life straight.
And rectifies herself
In making her outer action square.

When respecting and rectifying are established,
Then, fulfillment of virtue will be free from isolation.

"Straight, square, and great,
Not from learning.
Nothing is unfavorable."
It shows she has no doubt in what she does.

Although yin possesses beauty,
It is concealed.
Engaging in a king's service,
Claims no credit for herself.

This is the Tao of Earth,
The Tao of a wife,
And the Tao of one who serves the king.
The Tao of Earth is to make no claim on its own,
But, to bring everything to completion.

Changing and transforming of Heaven and Earth
Bring forth all plants flourishing.
If Heaven and Earth restrain their function,
Then an able person would withdraw from the light.
The I says, "Tie up a bag. No fault, no praise."
It counsels caution.

A superior person should hold the quality of Earth –
Yellow is central and moderate,
Understanding and considerate.
Correcting her position and perfecting her action,
Her beauty lies within.
It permeates her whole being
And manifests in all her doing.
This reveals the perfection of beauty.

When yin competes against yang,
A contest is certain.
Since no yang is considered,
Then a dragon is mentioned.
Since no category is changed,
The blood – a yin symbol – is noted.
Blue and yellow is Heaven and Earth in fusion.
Heaven is blue, Earth yellow.

9
九大德卦
Nine Hexagrams for Character Formation

Allocating a whole chapter of his writing – the seventh chapter of The Great Treatise – Confucius selected nine hexagrams, among the sixty-four, expounding specifically on character formation. He did this with the purpose of lifting the general mood of the people, elevating their sense of morality and rectifying their attitudes towards each other.

Tirelessly and earnestly, Confucius illustrated the nine hexagrams three times over. His purpose was to prevent moral degeneration. As a Chinese saying goes, "Repair the roof before it rains 未雨绸缪." His purpose was to prevent people from losing their personal integrity when positioned in disadvantageous situations.

The beginning of the seventh chapter states,

> *Did the I experience an upsurge in the middle antiquity?*
> *易之兴也其于中古乎?*
> *Did those who composed the I have experiences of sufferings and miseries?*
> *作易者其有忧患乎?*

These two inquiries referred to the rise of the I Ching of the Zhou Dynasty in the middle antiquity, close to the end of the Shang dynasty (or perhaps during the period at the intersection of the Shang and the Zhou dynasties). Confucius notes fear that those who composed the I Ching might have experienced great sufferings and miseries.

It was said that when Confucius studied the I Ching, he wore out the leather thongs, which fastened the bamboo tablets of the book, three times. He wrote The Commentaries to explain the I Ching and thus the Ten Wings came into existence.

King Wen and his son, the Duke of Zhou, as well as the common people, had withstood extreme difficulties during the period at the intersection of the Shang and the Zhou dynasties. It was known that while King Wen and the Duke of Zhou composed the I Ching, they had encountered great sufferings and miseries.

Those who made these reflections worried about how to prevent letting personal integrity slip in such a sorrowful plight. They felt themselves in sympathy with the authors in this respect. For those people too, they could do nothing more than preserve for posterity the framework of a perishing civilization.

The First Statement of Confucius on Character Formation

Confucius states,

> *Thus the hexagram Fulfillment* 履 *(10) shows the foundation of character* 德之基也; *Humbleness* 謙 *(15) reveals the handle of character* 德之柄也; *Turning Back* 复 *(24), is the root of character* 德之本也; *Long Lasting* 恒 *(32) brings about the firmness of character* 德之固也; *Decreasing* 損 *(41), is the cultivation of character* 德之修也; *Increasing* 益 *(42), the fullness of character* 德之裕也; *Exhausting* 困 *(47), the test of character* 德之辨也; *Replenishing, The Well,* 井 *(48), the field of character* 德之地也; *and Proceeding Humbly* 巽 *(57), the exercise of character* 德之制也.

Fulfillment 履, building the foundation of character 德之基也, is the first step of character formation. It signifies walking forward cautiously. It embodies the meaning of following the norms of propriety. In doing so, one would not turn against the social norms. Thus, it is the foundation of character formation. 履 Lu, in Chinese, is "doing," "performing," "fulfilling" and "carrying out." It is learning by doing. With regards to character formation, one should devote much time and energy to practicing and doing.

Humbleness 谦, being modest, is the handle of character 德之柄也. It is the key to character formation. Acting morally without practicing humbleness is like morality without a handle. The operation of an axe or a knife relies on its handle. In getting along with people humbly and modestly, one gets respect from people, thus enhancing character formation further.

Turning Back 复, reviving, is the root of character 德之本也. It contains the meaning of turning back to the right way. *The Great Learning* 大学 says, "On the bathing tub of Tang, the following words were engraved: 'If you can one day improve yourself, do so day by day. Yea, let there be daily self-improvement.' 苟日新, 日日新, 又日新." If one is able to turn back to the correct way, it becomes the root cause of improving one's virtue and refining one's intention. A stream has its source and a tree has its root. One should continuously break away from external bad influences, returning back to one's own innate, virtuous nature. This is the root of character formation.

Long Lasting 恒, being constant, is persistence of character 德之固也. It embodies the meaning of enduring, which reminds people to always be alert so that character building never stops. It should be carried through from the beginning to the end of life, without interruption. If one persistently relies on following the right path, a sense of morality will be long lasting.

Decreasing 损, discarding evil, is the cultivation of character 德之修也. Confucius says, "What truly is within will be manifested without. Therefore, the superior man must be watchful over himself when he is alone. 诚于中, 形于外, 故君子必慎其独也." One should discard those things harmful to character formation and absorb those things beneficial to it.

Increasing 益, absorbing the good, is the fullness of character 德之裕也. It contains the meaning of bestowing favors on other people. If one is able to bestow favors on other people, one is able to amplify oneself. Confucius says,

"When I walk along with two others, they may serve me as my teachers. I will select their good qualities and imitate them, recognize their bad qualities and avoid them. 三人行, 必有我师焉, 择其善者而丛之, 其不善者而改之." The goal of character formation is to increase one's virtues daily, making one's virtue more than sufficient.

Exhausting 困 means "tired out." This represents the test of character 德之辨也. Adversity reveals one's virtue. Only during the time of year when it becomes severely cold do we recognize that the pine and the cypress are the last to lose their leaves 岁寒知松柏之後凋. Likewise, only in a difficult circumstance can one distinguish one's morality. After facing adversity and falling into dire straits, one is able then to identify how solid one's virtues are.

Replenishing, The Well 井, represents the field of character 德之地也. One of the distinguishing features of a well is that it replenishes itself, thereby constantly serving the people who use it, without changing its nature. One's moral character should always compel one to be good to others and, like the well, never change one's essential nature.

Proceeding Humbly 巽, being modest, is the exercise of character 德之制也. The behavior of a person of integrity should not rigidly adhere to formalities. He should take measures suited to the time and the situation. On the other hand, one should not follow one's own preferences. Confucius said, "Though a man has abilities as admirable as those of the Duke of Zhou, yet if he be proud and ungenerous, those other attributes are really not worth considering. 如有周公之才之美，使骄且吝，其余不足观也已"

Actually, the whole book, including all sixty-four hexagrams in the I Ching is guidance on moral establishment. But these particular nine are basic and fundamental, which is why Confucius concentrated on them to educate the public on character formation.

The first three hexagrams, Fulfillment, Humbleness and Turning Back represent the commencement of character formation. The second three, Long Lasting, Decreasing and Increasing are about making strict demands on oneself. The last three, Exhausting, Replenishing and Proceeding Humbly, are related to gaining experience from life.

The Second Statement of Confucius on Character Formation

The hexagram of Fulfillment is harmonious and attains its goal. Humbleness gives honor and shines forth. Turning Back is small, yet different from external things. Long Lasting shows manifold experiences without satiety. Decreasing shows first what is difficult and then what is easy. Increasing shows the growth of fullness without artifices. Exhausting leads to perplexity and thereby to success. Replenishing, The Well, abides in its place, yet has influence on other things. Through Proceeding Humbly one is able to weigh things and remain hidden.

Fulfillment 履 is being harmonious and attaining the goal. This hexagram deals with the norms of good conduct,; corresponding with good conduct is a prerequisite of good character formation. Good conduct is harmonious and hence attains its goal even under difficult circumstances.

Humbleness 谦 is being honorable and glorified. This hexagram reveals one's attitude, which is necessary before character formation begins. It teaches people to get along with others humbly and modestly.

Humbleness honors others and thereby attains honor for itself; it regulates human interaction in such a way that friendliness induces more friendliness. A humble person will be honored and their humbleness will be glorified.

Turning Back 复. This hexagram ䷗ is characterized by the fact that a firm element originates from below and rises upward. The firm is growing and expanding. It signifies that the root and stem of character formation are growing and expanding. It also indicates that, from a trivial omen, one can become aware of the balance of good and evil in a circumstance. In doing so, one is strong enough to be able to constantly prevail in one's own unique character against any temptation. In this sense, Turning Back also suggests that self-examination and self-knowledge are necessary to avoid committing errors. It guides people to return to the right way before it is too late.

Long Lasting 恒 means "mixed" but not "being tired of." "Mixed" indicates that evil and virtue are mixing. "Not being tired of" indicates not being tired of keeping to the right way. The Commentary on the Decision says, "It is favorable to go somewhere. An end is always followed by a new beginning." This hexagram brings about firmness of character in the frame of time. It instructs people to maintain righteousness constantly and never become weary of doing so.

Decreasing 损 difficulty at first, ease follows. This hexagram ☷ comes from Advance ☰ (11), representing a decrease of the lower trigram in favor of the upper – that is, that the third line, originally strong, has moved up to the top; and the top line, originally weak, has replaced it. It shows a decrease of the lower faculties, the untamed instincts, in favor of the higher life of mind. Here we have the essence of character training. The hexagram shows first the difficult thing – the taming of the instincts; then, the easy phase, when character is under control; thus harm is kept away.

Increasing 益. This means "abundant," but not artificially so. This hexagram gives needed fullness to character. The Commentary on the Decision says, "Increasing moves with gentleness and mildness. It proceeds daily without limit. Heaven bestows and Earth accepts. Thereby things increase without restriction." Mere self-discipline is not enough to create good character; greatness is also needed. Thus, Increasing shows a spontaneous growth of personality that is not artificial and hence furthers what is useful.

Exhausting 困 is being in an impasse but also unobstructed. The Commentary on the Decision says, "Facing danger, still optimistic. In an exhausting situation one does not lose one's prosperity and smoothness; although only the superior person is able to do this." This hexagram represents the individual of developed character finally being in an impasse, where he must prove himself. Difficulties and obstacles arise; these must be overcome; yet they often prove insurmountable. He sees himself confronted by bounds that he cannot set aside, but these can be overcome by recognizing them for what they are. In thus recognizing as fate the things that must be accepted, one ceases to hate adversity. Of what use would it be to resist against fate? Through this lessening of resentment, character is purified and advances to a higher level.

Replenishing, The Well 井. The Decision of the hexagram says, "The site of a village may be moved, but not the well. Neither losing nor gaining. Coming and going, drawing, drawing."

This hexagram represents a wellspring, which, though fixed in one spot, dispenses blessings far and wide so that its influence is far reaching. This shows the field in which character can take effect. We perceive the profound influence emanating from a richly endowed and generous personality, an influence that is not any the less because the person exerting it keeps in the background. The hexagram shows what is right, and thus makes it possible for righteousness to take effect.

Proceeding Humbly 巽 ䷸. The Commentary on the Decision says, "The symbol of Wind is doubled. It signifies to repeat one's command once more. The firm proceeds humbly to the central place and the correct position. Its goal is able to be fulfilled."

This hexagram illustrates the proper flexibility of character. What is required is not rigidly holding fast to established principles, but instead, mobility – guiding action along its course of development without exposing oneself like the wind. Thus, one weighs matters and penetrates to the need of the situation without exposing oneself to attack. In doing so, one learns to take circumstance into account and to persevere with a strong unity of character, along with intelligent versatility.

The above-mentioned comprise the second statement of the nine hexagrams, going a step further to illuminate their qualities.

The Third Statement of Confucius on Character Formations

Here is the third statement of Confucius on the nine hexagrams, explaining the way to deal with hardship.

> *Fulfillment brings about harmonious conduct. Humbleness serves to regulate the mores. Turning Back leads to self-knowledge. Long Lasting brings about unity of character. Decreasing keeps harm away. Increasing furthers what is useful. Through Exhausting one learns to lesson one's rancor. Replenishing, The Well, brings about discrimination as to what is right. Through Proceeding Humbly one is able to take circumstance into account.*

Fulfillment brings about harmonious conduct. Thus, a virtuous person will act according to the principle of equilibrium and harmony.

The Doctrine of the Mean 中庸 says, "Let the states of equilibrium and harmony exist in perfection. Thus, a happy order will prevail throughout Heaven and Earth, and all things will be nourished and thereby flourish. 致中和, 天地位焉, 万物育焉."

Humbleness serves to regulate the mores. Confucius says, "Superior person, humble, humble. 谦谦君子." As a prerequisite of etiquette, only virtuous persons are able to employ humbleness to guide their manners.

Turning Back leads to self-knowledge. A virtuous person examines his evil intentions and turns back to the good. The Commentary on the Yao says, "Turning back without going too far, one cultivates one's virtue. Sincerely turning back. Being central, he is able to examine himself."

Long Lasting brings about unity of character. The superior person is able to be virtuous consistently and never change; it represents bringing about unity of character.

Decreasing keeps harm away. Discarding ill intent is to keep out of harm's way. Decreasing is able to keep mischief away.

Increasing furthers what is useful. Increasing promotes what is beneficial. It benefits others as well as oneself. Having regard for all those involved in a situation, furthers what is useful.

Through Exhausting, one learns to lessen one's rancor. The superior person in encountering himself in a tight corner, extricates himself from a difficult position.

Replenishing, The Well, brings about discrimination as to what is right. Replenishing bestows favors on others without losing anything of oneself.

Through Proceeding Humbly, one is able to take special circumstances into account. It is weighing the advantages and disadvantages of the situation and seeing through the phenomena to grasp its essence. It is acting in submission to others without revealing one's own preferences.

Millennium Time Capsule Text by Master Alfred Huang, October 2000

Deep in my heart, I always hold faith in the future.

I believe with confidence, that the twenty-first century will be a century of seeking harmony and great harvest. Through seeking harmony, prosperity and affluence will be harvested in all nations. And eventually, international harmony and world peace will at last be reaped in the third millennium.

The nineteenth century was a century primarily of British influence. The twentieth century was a century primarily of American influence. I believe deeply, that the twenty-first century will be a century dominated by Chinese influence.

Furthermore, I believe firmly, that humanity is evolving to a higher level. After the physical and mental aspects of human evolution have reached a certain point, the evolution of the spiritual aspect will play a dominant role. According to the I Ching, after seeking harmony we will obtain a great harvest. After a great harvest, we will be most humble, and after being most humble we will be able to enjoy great delight. This is the spiritual journey of the whole of humanity.

The essence of the I Ching is THE UNITY OF HEAVEN AND HUMANITY, which teaches people TO ACT IN ACCORDANCE WITH THE WILL OF HEAVEN AND THE WISHES OF PEOPLE, equivalent to the Western idea of THY WILL BE DONE. The aspiration and vision of the Founding Fathers of America is A NEW ORDER OF ALL AGES, while that of China is that BETWEEN HEAVEN AND EARTH, PEOPLE ARE MOST IMPORTANT AND VALUABLE. The ancient sages instruct: BRINGING FORTH THE GREAT TAO, ALL THINGS UNDER HEAVEN BELONG TO THE PEOPLE. In 1911, when Dr. Sun Yet-sen launched the revolution to overthrow the Qing dynasty and establish the republic, he held aloft this aspiration and vision to mobilize the people. The Chinese sense of DEMOCRACY is PEOPLE ARE MASTERS. The Chinese sense of PEACE is HARMONY AND EQUALITY. All these insights originated from the I Ching. Since the I Ching is the source of Chinese culture, it has been rooted deeply in the subconscious of every Chinese for four or five thousand years.

The Chinese are a people filled with historic pride. They respect their heritage and honor their past. They firmly believe that their present is the outcome of the past, and their future will be the outcome of the present. The ideal society of the ancient Chinese was a society that would *"let all the elderly be well ended, all the strong be well used, all the young be well nourished, and all the disadvantaged, widowers and widows, orphans, elderly without children, disabled, and diseased be well cared for." "Even things which are disliked and discarded on the ground should not be kept for one's own use; strength resists being reserved in the body, but should not be used for one's selfish purposes."* Such a society was called DA TONG, literally: THE SOCIETY OF GREAT EQUALITY. It contained a primitive aspiration of the idea of communism. This kind of ideal society has inspired many Chinese thinkers, including Dr. Sun Yet-sen and some of the communist leaders, to reform their country.

Since THE SOCIETY OF GREAT EQUALITY had been lost due to self-ishness emerging in peoples' minds, many ancient books describe another kind of society called XIAO KONG; literally: THE SOCIETY OF MODEST PROSPERITY. As the books say: *"Now the Great Tao has withdrawn. Things under heaven belong to families . . ."* This kind of society had been practiced by King Yu of the Xia dynasty, King Tang of the Shang dynasty, and King Wen of the Zhou dynasty over thousands of years. All these were virtuous kings practicing magnanimous government and caring for the people.

Since 1840, China has been defeated and humiliated by Western capitalism and Japanese militarism, one after another. Progressives of China have devoted their lives to seeking a way to make China prosperous and strong. For over a hundred years, China has been a student of the West as well as of the East, both ending in failure. Being wounded by both, China learned lessons from bitter experiences and won wisdom from hard knocks. In seeking prosperity and strength, China had to proceed from her own reality and to work on a path of her own. Eventually China found her own way. That is, China's new democracy opens up the possibility of socialism with Chinese characteristics.

Socialism is a Western philosophy beginning with Karl Marx. Chinese culture originates from the I Ching. The purpose of socialism is to eliminate the poverty of the majority, while the essence of the Chinese culture suggests to the Chinese Communist Party to establish THE SOCIETY OF MEDIUM PROSPERITY before the middle of the twenty-first century, which then can advance to THE SOCIETY OF GREAT EQUALITY.

China has had a long tradition as a brilliant and peaceful country. I deeply believe **if** China truthfully follows the treasures of her culture to realize a socialism of Chinese characteristics, China will be a great influence over the world in the twenty-first century.

Epilogue

by Regina Sara Ryan

Generally, a book's author will write its Epilogue, but in this case I am privileged to have been invited by Master Alfred to handle the task. As his copy-editor, I came to this text with an open mind and great interest. However, my background or experience with I Ching was minimal at best. Once a year, during a week or two of reunion with my dear heart-friend Lalitha, who had studied I Ching and once met with Master Alfred, I would receive a reading. My questions usually amounted to such generic inquiries as "What should I observe within my life for the months ahead?"

Lalitha's readings for me became more precise as the years went by, and so I was first connected, even if several steps removed, with the wisdom of I Ching as expressed by this master. As a seeker of truth coming from a long history within both Christian and Hindu traditions, I found I Ching's orientation fascinating, but more than that, I appreciated that it was filled with compassion and balance.

Fortunately, an experienced editor does not need to be an expert in the subject matter of a text being edited. Clear sentence construction is clear sentence construction, and the savvy editor soon learns the jargon, the general sense of the author's intention, along with his or her habits and shortcomings— some writers are masters of redundancy, while others leave the reader in limbo, assuming more than a beginner would ever know.

I took the job of copy-editing Master Alfred's book with a bit of trepidation, but essentially with a desire to connect to such an experienced practitioner of this time-honored form and art. I wanted "in" with someone who knew something of lasting value. What better way to learn than to risk the humiliation of having to ask the most obvious questions — which I did, with a flourish! But Master Alfred and Dan Nesbitt had nothing but spaciousness for my naiveté. They both wanted genuine help to make the message clear and understandable, especially for a "newbie," as I was. Master Alfred was gracious and kind from start to finish.

The structure of the book took me on a journey. A certain sense of "boring down" into the bedrock of the discipline was slowly, inexorably, taking place for me. Without knowing it directly, and occasionally wondering if I was learning *anything* at all, I circled the great text, like one might circulate an old temple, with Master Alfred's gentle hand to guide me. And, to my enormous surprise, I found myself one day glimpsing a distant door, apparently to an inner chamber, that I didn't even know existed. While I certainly haven't entered that room, yet, I was soon asking questions that actually mattered, making distinctions that fed my contemplative heart, and being captivated by a philosophy of harmony suffused with a demand for rigorous self-honesty. *Understanding the I Ching* became an adjunct source of wisdom in a lifelong quest for what is real, true.

And now, like any beginner who finds the first taste sweet, I want to know what's next. As an editor also, I anticipate that you, dear reader, may share this question. The answer for both of us is the same. Master Alfred's seminal text, *The Complete I Ching*, is the place to go next, or to begin *again* if you already possess it, as many of you probably do. Use the I Ching for yourself, in the ways he recommends. Re-read this current book, circling the temple slowly and thoughtfully as I have. And, await his next book, *The Comprehensive I Ching*, with eagerness.

May this work serve you, and all; and may it serve to relieve suffering and bring the rain of harmony promised by the great ones of old to this parched, disordered world.

About the Author

"When I was sixteen years of age, Grandpa, my mentor, introduced me to the field of I Ching. He talked about six dragons flying in the sky and a mare galloping across the vast plain . . ."

Thus began an apprenticeship that would become a life work for Master Alfred Huang, who at ninety-three years of age is one of the foremost experts in the understanding of I Ching.

MASTER ALFRED HUANG was born in China in 1921. Having first received his grandfather's transmission of the I Ching, he continued these studies with some of China's greatest minds. This great source of wisdom was a banned book at that time, and he was branded as an antirevolutionary in

1957. First, he was forced into manual labor and then into imprisonment and sentenced to death in 1966 at the start of the Cultural Revolution. Throughout his years in prison Master Huang meditated on the I Ching and thus found the strength to survive. About these twenty-two years of confinement he writes: "The most valuable harvest … was relying on the Divine's guidance all the time." Released in 1979, and weighing only eighty pounds, he emigrated to the United States.

Master Huang is a former Dean of Students at Shanghai University, and currently a professor of Taoist philosophy and a third-generation master of Wu-style Tai Chi Chuan, Chi Kung, and Oriental meditation. The founder of New Harmony, a nonprofit organization devoted to self-healing, he is the author of *The Complete I Ching*, *The Numerology of the I Ching* and *Complete Tai-Chi*.

Master Huang lives on the island of Maui where he continues to write, teach and spread his message of Harmony.

Author photograph by Blaine Michioka